PORTRAIT OF EUROPE

SALVADOR DE MADARIAGA

PORTRAIT
OF
EUROPE

HOLLIS & CARTER

LONDON

To

Jeanne & Julius
Hoste

CONTENTS

PART IV

EUROPEAN RESONANCES

AUTHOR'S FOREWORD TO
NEW EDITION

As I read this book again after fourteen years, I wonder time and again at the number of events, big and small, which in this short lapse of time have come to roost just at the nests I had prepared for them. The very day I began to brood over these lines I am now writing, I heard the B.B.C. lunch announcements, "trailing" the day's programme, with a lusty "You Spanish dog". Yet another "Spanish Main" dramatized story of some encounter between a Spanish galleon and an English pirate ship. "Pirate", by the way, was the B.B.C.'s own choice of word, not mine. This interesting contribution to the integration of Europe we are all working for, or against, seemed to me a fitting comment on England–Spain.

It brought to my mind those stiletto heels that a bold fashion inflicted on women precisely during these years, until they succumbed (have they?) to the joint attack of orthopaedic doctors, carpet-menders and air lines—these last having declared that an elephant is less dangerous to an aircraft floor than a young woman standing on stiletto heels, because the pressure per square centimeter is much higher in her case than in that of the monumental animal. I need not point out, though I do so, that these stiletto heels came from

Italy, for this was shown in advance in my chapter on
Italy–France.

I am sorry about that square "centimeter". I should
have said square inch (if the stiletto heel ever reaches
that acreage, which is doubtful), for these fourteen
years have given forth a truly enjoyable stream of letters
to *The Times* in protest against the unseemly attempts of
the B.B.C. to lead the British people gently into the
decimal system by way of the centigrade thermometer.
It should have been obvious to the B.B.C. that to try
to induce Britons to count degrees of heat and cold by
a scale in which water freezes at o and boils at 100,
instead of one in which it freezes at 32 and boils at 212,
was little short of an insult. With a courage that must
be admired, the British government have decided to
decimalize their currency, having made sure that no
other nation in the world remains to do so after
Britain; but they have been careful to effect the change
so that the cent or new penny will have a half penny
running after it up and down the columns of the ledgers
and in and out of the levers or circuits of the cash
registers. At any rate I am proud to reprint here the
closing words which I wrote in 1952 for my chapter
on France–England: "And the English still refuse to
build that tunnel."

I am also proud to be able to confirm what I wrote
about how natural and at home Spaniards feel in the
bosom of absurdity and how easily they refuse to accept
reality as it is or as it thinks it is, by relating what
happened to a team of American missionaries who were
endeavouring to convert a Spaniard to their faith.
"How could you expect me to become a Protestant,"
argued the Spaniard, "when I don't even believe in the

Catholic religion which is the only true one?" Let me add that the last time I told that story to a liberal countryman of mine, he affirmed with some conviction: "That is exactly my stand."

I must respectfully thank General de Gaulle for having so dramatically and powerfully confirmed my chapter on France–England. A more direct confrontation of the evolution of Franco-British relations from 1952 to 1964 with my chapter France–England would be idle and might become a mere exercise in vanity. Nor is the French President the only protagonist who has deigned to conform to the views I had printed before he acted, since a similar acquiescence in my way of describing Anglo-French tensions has been wittingly or unwittingly expressed in deeds and words by many Britons of various degrees of prominence.

I should, however, refer to one aspect of things under which events may be moving away from my design of European psychology at least in its present-day form. In my chapter on Germany–England, I had endeavoured to detect the influence of German envy towards a Britain successful, powerful and imperial. I believe this force is still at work, but it may no longer be as strong as it was fourteen years ago. Since then, the world has seen the involution of the British Empire, and the so-called German miracle; while Britain is struggling with economic and financial difficulties known to all. It would be a mistake to imagine that the admiration, hidden or declared, which the average German feels for Britain and the British, has lost significantly in strength; but it may be that, at the national level, it no longer acts with as much vigour as I tried to describe it in my chapter on Anglo-German tensions.

Nor should I omit the blanket of American influence, colourful and picturesque on its top side, criss-crossed with ill-humoured strokes and scribbles of "yankee go home" on the reverse side, which has since covered all our continent and tends to obliterate its variety, possibly its sense of quality, I hope not its sense of humour.

Such changes are inevitable when dealing with living beings, and Europe is certainly one of them—let alone the fact that while on a subject as rich and vast as this, errors are bound to creep in. I am glad only two were pointed out to me at the time by my good-natured critics—neither of them weighty enough to force me to inflict a correction on the printer. *Erse*, which I put in Mr. de Valera's mouth in my chapter on the Irish should, Denis Brogan told me, be *Irish*; and I should not have interpreted certain melodies in *Die Meistersinger* as a satire on Mozart. Well, these are my two sins, which I confess; though I confess also that I do not feel very repentant about them. I wish, though, that I had been fairer to Voltaire, who is a bigger European, man and thinker, than I make him out to be in my chapter on the Swiss.

But of this kind of error there is no end; and it may be just as well, as is suggested most aptly by another Spanish story of the 1952–66 crop: a Spaniard from Spain, who had not even troubled to get naturalised, had somehow or other become a municipal councillor in a small Mexican city. He moved that a lamp post be erected at a rather dark spot in the town. The matter was debated at some length, and the mayor put the motion to the vote. Everyone voted *yes*; but when at last the mover's turn came, the Spaniard voted *no*.

Taken aback, the mayor reminded him of the fact that the motion was his. "Yes," answered the Spaniard, "but I hate unanimity."

SALVADOR DE MADARIAGA
Oxford, July 1966

B

PART I

THE SPIRIT OF EUROPE

1

LAND AND CLIMATE

MANY film-goers will remember that scene in *The Ghost Goes West*, when the American millionaire who has bought, shipped and rebuilt in Florida a Scotch medieval castle shows his acquisition to a friend, who, somewhat bewildered, asks: "But why that Venetian canal and that gondola in front of a Scotch castle?" And the American explains: "Well, don't you know? the European touch."

You laugh first; but if you are a true European, and no longer merely a Scotchman or a Venetian, the sally of the innocent American leaves you dreaming. Was he not seeing ahead of all of us, including the author of the script? At the distance at which he saw it, from Florida, a Venetian canal with its gondola, in front of a Scotch castle, was as natural for him as is for any of us the Scots Guards marching in the Mall—a sight which would have made a sixteenth-century Scot split his sides with laughter.

The stroke of genius is in that "European touch." For it is in the living sense of Europe that we shall find the secret of the unity under the variety of European life. Seen as a whole, Europe stands out in as clear a light as any of its component nations. The differences between Scandinavian and Teuton, Latin and Slav, are suffused into a general likeness, a family air more assertive and impressive than any of the shades and accents that give character and variety to the men and nations it unites; so that in the end, particularly when seen from another continent, the Venetian gondola and the Scotch castle do seem to us adequate companions and neighbours in a picture endowed by history and psychology with an impressive unity of its own.

We do, on reflection, return to the feeling of diversity; and our mind dwells again on the truly marvellous wealth of national types our little Europe has brought forth; from the burly, slow Swede to the mercurial and swift Frenchman; from the fiery Irishman to the subtle Greek, from the empirical Englishman to the uncompromising Pole, from the practical and placid Swiss to the keen, aesthetical Italian, from the gregarious but arrogant German to the rebellious Iberian; and right across these frontiers of character, the inexhaustible varieties of physical type, stature, colour of hair, skin and eyes, in inextricable and innumerable combinations. And yet, this variety is no chaos; but rather, despite this wealth of types and a considerable turbulence in their deeds, a unity again which forces itself upon the mind, and says: *This is Europe.*

A similar variety within unity impresses the mind that beholds that peculiarly European treasure—its cities. When our memory wanders from Uppsala to Seville, from Bath to Cracow, from Chartres to Budapest, from Copenhagen to Siena; when we close our eyes to see the leafy trees of a street in Amsterdam placidly reflected on the liquid fairway; or the sun paint in vivid colours the splendours of Naples; or the parallel lines of elegant poplars meander with the Loire from château

to château; or the Alhambra raise above Granada its
walls and gates steeped in nostalgy for the Moors; or
Coimbra listening to her convent bells in scholarly
quietness; or Salzburg dream of its Mozartian days;
when we behold all the beauty which our European
cities have crystallized in the course of time, it is again
their marvellous variety and yet their no less marvellous
unity which remain as the lasting impressions in our
mind.

The first and most natural cause of this unity and
variety of Europe is its physical environment. This
smallest of all Continents, a feature of the world hardly
more important than a cape or promontory of Asia, is,
to begin with, endowed with an equable temperature,
higher than that of American and Asiatic zones of similar
latitude. Europe owes this advantage to her remarkable
heating systems; and I say "systems" in plural, ad-
visedly; for lavish nature has provided our continent
with two of them: one comparable to the old-fashioned
Spanish *brasero*, and the other to the modern hot-water
boiler. The *brasero* is the Sahara, where the winds get
hot that keep warm the whole South of Europe. The
heel of Italy stands at a latitude slightly north of Philadelphia; but while in Philadelphia the river freezes in
winter, no one in Otranto has seen ice outside his glass
of vermouth. Not content with drawing thus as much
warmth as possible from the continent just across the
narrow Mediterranean to warm our little Europe, nature
managed to set up a system to draw a good deal of heat
for the same purpose across the Atlantic, from distant
America, without even waiting for the New World to
be discovered by that Europe it was to keep warm.

This contrivance is known as the Gulf Stream, and amounts to a hot-water central-heating system whereby the water held in the Gulf of Mexico is heated by the tropical sun till the action of physical laws brings it across the Ocean to raise the temperature of all Western Europe, from Portugal to Norway. Britain, in particular, owes to this central-heating the moderate climate it enjoys instead of the ice-bound life it would have to endure on account of its latitude and exposure to the polar winds.

This mere fact, along with the historical consequences it implies, shows the importance of the Gulf Stream. How dramatic stands out the stubborn search of the Spaniards for a passage across Darien to the South Sea. Had such a passage existed the water in the boiler for the Gulf Stream would have leaked through that passage, thus destroying the central heating for Western Europe, and possibly, by radically altering the climate, the stock and the history of Spain, which would have made it impossible for those Spaniards to have gone there at all! It was the New World after all, that, from behind the veil of distance, was determining the European conditions that would allow the Europeans to discover it. That narrow strip of land which connects the Northern to the Southern part of America turns out to be a key feature, not only of the New but of the Old World as well; for without it the Gulf Stream would not have existed; Spain, France and England would have been much colder countries, and the history of the world, which these three nations have powerfully contributed to shape, would have taken a different course.

Heating, of the *brasero* and of the hot-water type, is not, however, the only cause of the privileged climate of

Europe. The shape of the continent is in itself favourable
to moderate temperatures. The crystalline mass of the
Scandinavian Peninsula protects the mainland from the
full blast of the frozen polar winds; and a series of high
table lands and chains of mountains running east-west
(instead of north-south as they do in America) contributes further to honeycomb the Continent with regions
of mild climate free from the rigours of the North.

This equidistance from extremes is a general feature
of physical Europe. Her rivers are neither big nor small;
her mountains do not rise beyond rather more than half
the height of the Himalayas or the Andes. Her plains are
limited; her valleys shapely and small; and her coasts
are so deeply indented that every sea becomes a kind of
hearth for a family circle.

A glance at the map is enough to account for that unity
and that variety which impress the observer of Europe
at first sight. Unity comes from the relatively short
limits of climate and configuration within which the
life of Europe has to flow; variety from the many nooks
and corners looking south, north, east, west, which the
mountains, seas and rivers of the Continent offer to its
inhabitants.

The inhabitants themselves, by their blood, contribute
to this unity and this variety in a way of their own. The
scientific approach to this vexed subject has destroyed
many a fairy tale. Broadly speaking, there are three
European types known by names derived from their
chief abodes: the Nordic, tall, long-headed, light-eyed
and long-nosed; the Eurasiatic, middle-sized, broad-
headed, light-eyed and short-nosed; and the Mediterranean, short, long-headed, dark-eyed and long-nosed.

This simplicity, however, is but simplification. Europeans are above all a mixed lot; other types, such as the Dinaric, tall and dark, the Celt, some Mongoloids, and, of course, the omni-present Jews, not to speak of the pre-historic elements which linger on from bygone ages, come to complicate the colours of the palette; but the brush of history has worked hard with them through the centuries, so that to-day there is no nation in Europe able to say: "Behold, a pure race."

How fortunate indeed for Europe! Strange as it may sound first, this mixture of different human stocks is perhaps the true cause of European unity; but I shall not attempt to solve this paradox till the picturesque landscape of European variety has been adequately surveyed.

For the true "stocks" of Europe are not those that science describes with indexes of size and colour for skull, hair and eyes; but the definite varieties which the years and the centuries have grown with a number of combinations of these scientific types, by nursing them in the wonderfully different environments of the European soil and climate. The score of "cups" set by nature in the nooks and corners of Europe have received successive waves of these elementary stocks at different times and in different doses; and by the creative interaction of man and environment, they have evolved a score of European peoples which are the true living realities of Europe. Nordic, Eurasiatic, Mediterranean and Dinaric are all very well for biology; for history and for life, let us have Englishman, Frenchman, Spaniard, Italian, Pole and Swede. We can afford to smile at those who warn us that such terms are not *scientific*. What do we care? All we can answer is: "Sorry for science."

Are "Sherry", "Claret", "Burgundy" and "Tokay"

scientific terms? Chemical analysis dares not take on the task of defining them. But there are dons in Oxford who can tell any brand of them with an infallibility they would be too modest to assume were they to be confronted with an unlabelled Virgil or Euripides.

The chief virtue of Europe, her main gift to the world, is this capacity for producing *vintages* of national types with a strong spiritual and historical aroma of their own. It is in vain that matter-of-fact minds attempt to deny the existence of national characters. One of their favourite arguments consists in pointing out that at different times the same people have had different reputations and probably different characters; that, for instance, Elizabethan Englishmen were outspoken and uninhibited while Victorian Englishmen were reserved and inhibited. Well, what of it? As if a character could exist without changing or indeed change without existing. No. Let colour-blind people deny the rose and the carnation; Europe, for all that, remains rich above all in national characters. And these, not the measurable types and sub-species of biology, are the true components of the European spirit.

These significant differences of variety within a relatively narrow field of unity account for the typically European gift of *quality*. The essence of quality is uniqueness. Something, somebody has quality when it is different from the rest of a group in a peculiar and undefinable way, when, in other words, it can, at a glance, be singled out and, as the saying goes, *distinguished* from the rest. *Quality* and *distinction* are thus seen to be naturally interrelated. These two words describe two valuable European virtues. Snobbery and class-consciousness have unfortunately cheapened and inflated both the words and the concepts. That most detestable idea and despicable word "exclusiveness" has been erected round *quality* and *distinction* to isolate them from true life. But neither distinction nor quality has anything to do with class; they have much to do with *breeding*.

For, as the case of Europe itself shows, breeding is indispensable to the fostering of quality. The potter infallibly turning up a perfect curve out of his clay by a mere caress of his hand is guided in his tiniest impulses by many generations of ancestors—and how many generations of idle dreamers enjoyed in silence the pageant of the world before Velázquez or Goya rose from their midst to give back to the world all the joy they had consumed!

That uniqueness of quality and of distinction can neither be defined nor analysed; it must be *tasted* in order to be known. *Taste* is therefore one of the most pronounced features of the European. Not necessarily good taste, but the tendency to appraise things by standards of taste. This faculty of the mind has been given in all our languages the same name we give to the sense active in our palate and tongue because, like physical taste, it enables us to enjoy the most intimate, lived and direct experience of the things of the world man can achieve; and because, both in the taste of the mind and in that of the body, the object which is being known is appraised accurately and fully, yet ineffably; and it becomes part of the knower, is, in other words, by him *assimilated*.

Unity, the stem, variety, the branches, quality, the flower, taste, the aroma, such is the symbolical tree of the spirit of Europe.

2

EUROPE AS WILL AND MIND

A MAN is a tree that has packed up its earth and roots
and got moving. His bowels are his earth; his blood, his
sap; his lungs, his foliage; his legs and spine, his trunk;
and it is by no mere caprice of the language that we
describe by the same word the central part of the human
body and that of the body of a tree. So much for man's
vegetative life. But man is a tree also in a spiritual sense;
though this may require a more attentive contemplation
of that wonder of nature we call a tree.

Some matter-of-fact persons (usually people of no
clear notions about either *matter* or *fact*) may deny that
a tree is spirit. Let them think it over; for as a *matter of
fact*, trees have characters just like human beings, and in
the same uncanny twofold way: collective and individual.
Collective character in trees is so clear that it defines
the species to our intuition as concretely as biological
features do to our intellect. Most of us know trees by
their character; few beside scientists know them for
their specific, scientific aspects to which they owe their
place in biology. Who can deny that the willow, the
silver birch, the cypress, the oak, express definite moods
of a Poet-God as clearly as *Othello* and *As You Like It*
express definite moods of Shakespeare? This capacity
for putting our minds in sympathy with a clear-cut

mood or attitude springs from the tree as a member of its species, and therefore establishes the collective character of such a species.

So far, collective character in trees—which we might parallel to national character in men. But there is a world of difference between willow and willow, birch and birch, oak and oak; and to the sympathetic observer, no two trees are alike, and every one bears on its trunk, branches and foliage the stamp of a peculiar, "personal" character, and of a single and original destiny in tune with its circumstances and surroundings. This, in its turn, naturally calls to mind the personal and individual character every man evinces within his national character.

By spreading before man the incomparable wealth and pageant of its trees, the Spirit that creates all things and keeps them alive suggests to us that trees are not to be taken for granted as if they were but one of the "properties" of the stage on which man struts about on the Earth; but that, on the contrary, there is a deep-lying brotherhood between trees and men, which men should consider and contemplate.

Now the tree's frame falls into three parts: the roots; the trunk; and the branches. Each of these three parts has a function and a way all its own. There is an impressive energy in the downward drive of the roots forcing their way into the earth, from the dark, unseen recesses of which they draw sustenance to feed the whole tree. In the forest, the roots of neighbouring trees make up a vast underground world, a plurality of pluralities working obscurely for the trunks and foliages above.

From this obscure plurality sunk in the dark earth, rises towards the air, the sun and the blue heavens, the impressive unity of the trunk. No anonymity; no obscurity about it. The trunk is so assertive, so single that it naturally assumes the representation of the whole tree; so that roots and branches seem but its accidents, appendices or developments. The trunk is the pillar of the tree's strength, the impersonation of the tree's individuality. It is thanks to the determined and patient will of the stem in growing out of the seed along the radius of the earth, *i.e.*, by the shortest line towards the zenith (an impressive symbol, indeed, of man's ambition), that the tree exists at all and conquers for itself a space in the sun and a plot on the earth.

But what would all this unity be for and how could it exist at all if it did not splay and diversify itself again into the foliage? And so, the tree reproduces in mid-air, in the sun, and towards the sky that pattern which its roots had developed in the dark underground towards the depths. The tree is then up to a point a symmetrical construction: in the centre, its individualized, unitary and personal trunk; downwards and upwards, branches of diversity seeking to dissolve its unity into the common, anonymous, obscure earth and into the luminous sky where all tends to the sun.

How human all this is! Nature seems to echo the words uttered a few minutes ago: "A man is a tree that has packed up its earth and roots and got moving." And, like a tree, man is symmetrical: in the centre, his individual, unitary and personal self; downwards and upwards, branches of diversity seeking to dissolve his unity into the common, anonymous past of his ancestral earth, bowels, blood plasma; and in the luminous sky where all tends to the spirit.

All this has always been more or less obscurely felt, expressed and acted upon by human beings. The language hints at it in such sayings as that "man has a twig of craziness" or "a twig of poetry"; or again in the universal and time-honoured tradition which decorates with horns the deceived husband's brow. Religious painters have consecrated the spiritual character of the area surrounding the head, *i.e.*, the human "foliage" in the golden aura of the saints. And let us now remember manes of hair, lion-like or like the wind-swept leafy top of a tree, or brushed up, military fashion in lines of bayonets, dishevelled or carefully oiled and combed, wigs with all they suggest in their different shapes, between the flowing majesty of the Louis XIV period and the impertinent wit of the Louis XV, and above all hats. For of all garments, the hat is the most plastic to the spirit. It is in the hat that the spiritual foliage of man is expressed at its best. Identical models from the self-same shop soon take on different airs according to the heads that wear them. As for women's hats, comment would be too easy; one story may do, even though well known—that of the clergyman's wife entering a Paris shop to purchase *un chapeau bien chaste; c'est pour la femme d'un curé!* Chaste, she wanted it, and rightly because there are chaste hats, as there are frivolous or even obscene ones. But she failed to realize that the chastity or otherwise of a hat could not be bought in a shop; for, in point of hats, the moral features must be supplied by the wearer. Let a Spanish "Cordobés" hat be put on the head of a puritan woman, and the cold wind of the puritan head will put out the Spanish flame; while a fiery woman may set ablaze a whole bullring of spectators wearing a civil guard hat.

As for men's hats, the omnipresent Homburg, which

drove off the bowler which had driven off the top-hat,
takes on the spirit of the wearer with a willing docility.
The spendthrift and the miser, the churl and the nobleman, the large-minded and the meticulous, the bourgeois
and the bohemian, the city man and the artist, the
gloomy and the gay, all the forms and ways of the human
mind will express themselves in the form and the wing
and the pose and the air a hat will take in a few weeks
or even days. The same hat on an Arab will turn into a
turban, on a Japanese it will take the forward slant of
the headwear of the Samurai.

It is in the foliage of the tree that nature performs one
of its most wonderful miracles; the one, by the way, on
which all life on earth depends: the transmutation of
the energy of the sun into chemical energy to turn
carbon dioxide into sugar. So, that eagerness, that
single-mindedness and that single-willedness of the
plant's stem in seeking the light by growing in a straight
line towards the zenith, has its root-cause in a mysterious
faculty of the leaf to turn light into sustenance. And,
here again, how human all this is: the individual trunk
of man is supported by a downward, hidden, earthbound diversity; and seeks a higher sustenance in the
upward diversity of a foliage rising towards the light.

But, Sir, you were supposed to be talking about
Europe! Yes, of course, I was; a Europe thick with
human trees; every one of them with as strong a stem
of will and mind as any continent ever saw, for—and
here comes the fruit of this long digression among the
trees—every continent has its own peculiar way of
growing trees. The American continent must be left
aside in this disquisition, for in America man has played
havoc with nature like a bull in a china shop; but as for

c

the other three, it is clear that the stress is on the roots in Africa, on the foliage in Asia, and on the stem in Europe. And surely this observation deserves a few minutes' scrutiny. The roots are the obscure past, the blood-plasma and its memories, garnered and pooled by the vast commonalty of our ancestors, all churned together into one sap in the intertwining, throughout the centuries, of our family-trees. It is in that part of the human tree that the African continent is strong. The foliage of man is that light and airy part of his being which seems able to draw inspiration and intuition from the light above him. It is a part of the human tree particularly strong, in Asia, whence Europe has derived most of its religious notions and experiences. Europe is strongest in the stem; the one individualized part of the human tree on which the structure stands, as a well-defined unit of life, the conscious mind and will.

The reason why this is so might well be found in the play of unity and diversity which is typical of Europe. The "cups" into which it is divided by nature are definite enough, separate enough, for historical and psychological types or human vintages to be fostered and nurtured; but the obstacles between them are not so formidable as not to allow active relations of trade, friendship and war. This double circumstance endows Europe, on the one hand, with well-defined varieties of human beings, on the other, with a considerable number of blends between them. It follows that in the course of fifteen centuries of history, the Europeans have developed a rich mixture of bloods. All Europeans are mixed, and particularly those belonging to the urban populations. All, therefore, carry on in their inner beings a permanent dialogue between the several blood-

memories that live in them. The variety of Europe gives
to each of the "characters" in this inner conversation
enough definiteness and richness for the discussion to be
lively; the unity of Europe, on the other hand, preserves
enough common ground and reduces enough the distance
between the inner voices, for the discussion to be
stimulating and fertile. It is this perennial argument ever
going on in the recesses of the European being which has
determined the remarkable evolution of the European
intellect; since the intellect, like all forms of life, is
stimulated by exercise. That is why also the European
has evolved a strong differentiated will, since the will is
but the primal vital impulse made conscious by the mind.

Such might well be the reason why, while Asia yearns
towards heavenly things and Africa remains sub-earthly
and animistic, Europe disperses its being into myriads of
separate human stems, and prefers to express its genius
in terms of individuals. The individual is in fact a European discovery—if not a European invention. It is in
Europe that the peculiar unique character of the individual is first appreciated; and that again may well
explain why Christianity was predestined from the first
to become the specific religion of the Europeans. For,
with Christianity, the sacred character of every man is
recognized, no matter his class, wealth, craft or colour;
and this recognition, proclaimed on spiritual grounds,
calls forth a harmonious response from the individualistic
depths of the European soul. The will, one of the two
aspects of the master faculty of the European, feels itself
free to act in a world in which all individuals are declared
sacred; and from this liberation of the will springs the
exceptional activity of the European and the leading
share Europe takes in human history.

The other aspect of Europe's master faculty is the mind. And here also European history was bound to seek through its many vicissitudes that freedom of enquiry without which the mind can no more work than the lungs can breathe without air. Christian in its will, Europe is Socratic in its mind. Montaigne was never less European than when he coined that famous quip that doubt was a wondrous soft pillow for a well-made head. For the true European, doubt is not a soft pillow, but a spring-board for mental action; and when he struggles —as he has done throughout history and is doing now more than ever—when he struggles for his right to doubt, it is for his right to know that he is struggling.

Mental action, desire to know, are living aspects of man in which the mind and the will can be seen at play in an inseparable combination. The European mind is not especially contemplative, as is, for instance, the Asiatic. For the European, contemplation is the mother of appetite. The European mind is but a subtler eye; as the eye is but a subtler hand. The mind of the European contemplates in order to understand—but that act, understanding, is for the European so possessive and acquisitive that he expresses it in every language with images drawn from the possessive gestures of his hand. The European mind *grasps*, *seizes*, *apprehends*, *gets hold of an idea*, *catches a meaning*. This choice of words reveals a particularly active mind. It explains the unique position attained by the Europeans in the History of Knowledge.

The obverse of this faculty is a somewhat defective development of the intuitional gift. Strong in its trunk, the European tree is not as richly endowed in its foliage.

That is why Europe has always imported its religions
from the East. For the European to believe in an idea, it
must first have passed through the filter of his intellect.
This also explains why in Europe religions tend to shed
their purely devotional aspects and to develop into
doctrine—intellect—and into ethics—will. The Christian religion has been no exception to this rule; it also
has tended to become a dogmatic and doctrinal construction and a set of principles of behaviour mostly for
social use. But in so far as it emphasizes the sacred
character of every individual, it has saved the most
precious of the teachings of Christ. That is why the
ideal of the European—though often sinned against—is
a conscious and self-possessed unit of life, advancing in
the realms of knowledge warily and in a state of Socratic doubt, but in the realms of action resolutely, in
a spirit of Christian love.

3

THE THREE-IN-ONE RHYTHM

THIS, then, is the key feature of all European life and history: the predominance of the will and the mind over other forms of the spirit of man. Now, it is in the nature of things that the impulse at the root of the will should spring up first, mind coming on the stage later. We may, therefore, expect to observe in the life of the European a peculiar rhythm founded on this delay between the immediate will and the somewhat tardy mind-attack, reflection, summing up. In purely intellectual affairs this three-in-one rhythm gives rise to the group analysis-hypothesis-synthesis. In other forms, it is discernible also in every walk of European life. Thus, in social and political life, this three-in-one rhythm dominates the typical European struggle between the individual (attack), society (reflection) and liberal democracy (summing-up). Europeans are the inventors of individualism—a synthesis of the Socratic and the Christian traditions; but a mere individualism can lead to nought but anarchy, unless tempered by social considerations. As the impulse in the will has had its say, putting forward the individual, the tardy mind reflects and speaks for social considerations. The European then seeks to sum up retaining both, in a balanced combination of individual freedom and social discipline. Hence the essentially-un-European character of all doctrines in which either the first phase (anarchism) or the second phase (communism) predominates.

A similar rhythm will be observed in European imperialism. It is nearly always born of a purely individual impulse in which the European State has no share, to which, indeed, it may happen to be inimical. Cortés and Pizarro, Clive and Rhodes, were above all individuals who sallied forth on their own, moved by some obscure prompting for action. But in every case, after the conqueror had set his foot on the foreign land, the constructive move of reflection came to organize the filial State; and finally, as the summing-up, an independent State is built in imitation of the metropolitan one.

Such is also the rhythm of that typically European creation, science. First the mind "attacks" things and events, in an endeavour to *seize* or *apprehend* them through analysis; a phase of reflection follows, in which the mind builds up a net of ideas (a hypothesis) to catch the facts and objects and reduce them to man's order; and finally, as, here and there, the facts and objects may resist man's effort, a third phase of synthesis follows, in which the mind comes to terms with nature and readjusts its net the better to catch her.

It is this three-in-one rhythm of the European spirit, due to the delay between the coming into action of the instant will and the tardy mind, that lies under most of the human events which dialecticians have endeavoured to force into the Procrustean bed of materialistic or even of Hegelian dialectics. There is no theoretical or philosophical pattern above them; there is a psychological pattern underneath.

4

THE ARTS

THIS play of wit and will rules also the arts of Europe, and explains their chief characteristics; the geometrical simplicity and anthropomorphic proportions of its architecture; the predominance of the human figure, and particularly of the portrait, in the plastic arts, and the supremacy of its music.

Europe has given forth a wonderful variety of architectural forms, over which rise with unrivalled splendour the Greek and the Gothic. So varied is European architecture that at first it would seem impossible to reduce its many forms to a general law. There are, however, two such laws which both include all European architecture and exclude those of other (older) continents: symmetry and a certain harmony between its proportions and those of the human body. This twofold characteristic is subtly connected with the Socratic-Christian nature of the European spirit: inquisitive and analytical, the European, inventor of those two marvels, Euclidean and analytical geometry, begins its architectural adventures drawing the two axes, vertical and horizontal, which represent the soil on which it is to build and the direction along which the building is to rise. The European sense of order does the rest, and so the building rises with simple lines and relations between the masses on either side of the axes. Deeply conscious of the human standard for all things, the individual architect subdivides his building in harmony with the proportions of the human body.

This simplicity and this humanistic sense of form are manifest also in European sculpture. None of those elaborate pieces in which Indian, Chinese, Aztec artists have cast their dreams or symbols—gods with several arms, or with necklaces of hearts or human entrails—none even of those Egyptian deformations so striking in their hieratic poise. The European is simple and humble. He sculpts what is there as it is there. And it is on that simplicity that he builds up his work, trusting to sheer power without the help of those extraneous means. True, in recent times, the European has strayed from this exacting rule—but, in so far as he has forsaken the outwardly simple he has lost the inwardly complex, and become less European.

It is now clear why European painters excel in the portrait. The portrait is to the plastic arts what individualism is to sociology. In the portrait, the European painter expresses the mind and the will, and asserts the value of all men. When Rembrandt devotes his brushes to painting unforgettably the face of a Jewish rabbi, he says: "A Jew is for me as good as a Christian". When Velázquez, with the brush that painted Philip IV, paints the King's fools, he says: "For me a fool is as good as a King". These European painters have been the greatest humanists of Europe, the keenest seers into the heart of man, of any man. And when they have approached religious subjects, they have brought heaven to earth, and (perhaps with the one exception of El Greco) made God in the image of man, humanized the unfathomable mystery of His silence, and given men a respite in the hope that the Spirit that shapes all things may understand them.

Will and mind are welded to the present time more closely than instinct, which works from the past, or intuition, that searches the future—hence the supremacy of music in European life, and the supremacy of European music in History. Great as are the achievements of Europe in science and the plastic arts, as well as in literature, it is perhaps in music that our continent excels most.

Music is the art of time. It is also the art of action. From action it distils the subtlest essence and transmutes it into beauty. There is an original silence. Then the melody attacks. We enter into a state of tension, directed towards a future we feel in the coming, as yet unheard, notes, in the form of a melody or melodic prolongation which we do not know yet but guess obscurely; and so we advance along a line in which we feel some inner logic until the cadence leads us to the balance of silence again. How deep the sympathy between this process and that of our action, attacking the void outside to set in motion some happening with its reactions, obstacles, climaxes and finally a resolution and an end. As the transmutation of will into form and beauty, music is the most European of the arts.

It becomes doubly European when to this first faculty of representing the will in action, music adds that of evoking the mind. It would be venturesome to attempt a definition of the time and manner when music becomes a manifestation of the mind as well as an expression of the will of man. (Let us first dismiss as irrelevant all assimilations of this question to that of programme or descriptive music, such as that dreadful bird in the Sixth Symphony, an inferior sort of mind-music even in the hands of Beethoven.) After all, there is mind in all will worth the name. But it may be said that, as music evolves from the polyphonic to the melodic stage, the mind element rises more and more clearly. It is already triumphant in Johann Sebastian Bach. Haydn may perhaps be credited with the invention of that melodic language which, raised to perfection by Mozart, will enable Beethoven to write a moving dirge in the Third, lyrical poetry in the Fourth and a tragic poem in the Ninth.

All this is supremely European. The great musicians of our Continent have given to the world masterpieces of the European ideal, which is a synthesis of the will and the mind, of the Dionysian and the Apollonian strains in man. Great is Shakespeare, but in him the creative impulse breaks the dams of the mind. Great is Goethe, but in him the dams of the mind hinder the free flow of the creative impulse. Great is Leonardo, but his mind seems at times to paralyse him on the edge of creation. Only the masters of music, Bach, Mozart, Beethoven, have mastered the flow of their creative lava and moulded it into beauty. Bach, in particular, the perfect synthesis of poet and mathematician, rises above Europe as the true exponent of its genius.

PART II

THE EUROPEAN OLYMPUS

1

EUROPEANS OF THE SPIRIT

PHILOSOPHERS rightly emphasize the vigour of European traditional thought; historians, the might and majesty of the flow of European history; but artists are on even stronger ground than either of them in pointing to the world of European immortals as the highest, richest and brightest source of European consciousness and life. Thanks to her great creative spirits, Europe has evolved, in the course of ages, an Olympus of ever-living men and women, a sublimated and abiding Europe, ever moving on the screen of the mind. There, on the background of thoughts and memories, of the philosophy and the history of Europe, the great Europeans of the mind move and live, evolving as we do, and acting on us and on each other with the inner virtue left pulsating in them by the artists who created them. They are our gods. But while the Greeks made gods of the forces of nature, of the manifestations of FATE which they could not master, and had therefore to placate, we Europeans have given forth our Gods by endowing with human features and sap the tensions of our own complex and ever-labouring souls. Born of a mixture of bloods, carrying in his veins a moot of several collective memories, the European is a living debate, a permanent and never settled argument. It is this debate and this argument which our great creative artists have sublimated into an Olympus of European characters, Hamlet, Don Quixote, Faust, Don Juan, Ivan Karamazov, Peer Gynt. . . . There is a world of difference, for instance, between Don Juan's all too human adventures with the women he betrays and the hardly divine pranks of Jupiter with Danae and the rest. Jupiter is a god behaving like a human being, or, as Voltaire would have said, a god made in man's image out of reciprocity: Don Juan is a man who dons immortality by incarnating that which is *donjuanish* in all men. Such a transfiguration could hardly have happened without Christianity. Men there were always. Man begins with Christ. The new fact which transforms our history when Christ enters it is not that he, a man, claimed to be the son of God; but that He, a god, claimed to be the son of Man. By thus creating man, He made all men as vast, deep and everlasting as all mankind; and therefore opened to our poets a human space out of Space and a human time out of Time in which to launch these gods of ours which are all men, yet live permanently.

Of these our gods, Don Juan, Don Quixote, Hamlet and Faust are the greatest. But there are others: Ivan Karamazov for instance, or Peer Gynt; none, however, as universal as the four great ones. And it is worth noticing that out of the four, two are Spanish, while there are none who hail from either Italy or France. Strange at first, this fact reveals itself as normal and natural on reflection. France and Italy are the two mothers of European civilization; two countries whose contribution to Europe is almost unrivalled. Yet neither in French nor in Italian literary history is it possible to find immortal human beings such as Spain, England, Germany, Russia, Norway have given forth. Despite the marvellous fertility of Balzac, none of his characters towers high enough to enter the European Olympus. The puzzle may be resolved by considering not the shortcomings but the gifts of France and Italy. The vigour of the plastic sense, which is Italy's gift, will guide us to find in the Gioconda of Leonardo and the Moses of Michelangelo fit companions for our great Europeans of the spirit: while France, the mother of form and the giver of rules, provides the frame, the house, the stage, in which our great figures dwell. As for the figures themselves, they rise from realms of darkness and irrationality rarely visited by the luminous genius of France and Italy; and must therefore spring to the light of day in nations more familiar with the obscure valleys, the battling seas and the mysterious forests of the human soul.

Hence their vital force. For though every one of them is endowed with a vigorous power of symbolization, Hamlet, Faust, Don Quixote and Don Juan are not symbols; they are persons, carrying about that enigmatic air which all human beings really alive manage to convey. Enigmas on legs, like every one of us, whose unity is rather of the body than of the soul, and of the world of appearances and plastic forms rather than of that vast backworld of impulses, thoughts and intuitions which behind and beyond the clearest eyes fades away towards unimaginable horizons. Contradictory yet consistent, rich in shades of meaning and linked up to their world of men and things by a delicately modulated *chiaroscuro*; yet unmistakably clear in outline, gesture and style, these men of the spirit are perfectly known to us; yet when we try to analyse our acquaintance with them, we discover that what we mean by "knowing them" is that we know exactly the specific way in which every one of them is

unknown to us. We realize that we know neither the
enigma of Hamlet nor the enigma of Don Quixote; but
we know that they are different enigmas; and we have a
definite, clear feeling as to the shape and profile of the
one and of the other; the edges and corners wherewith
they touch us and act on our own enigma within. Thus
the glory of their creators turns out to be the power to
set up concrete and definite mysteries which we can
recognize at a glance and know from each other though
never in themselves.

These three factors—their inner vitality, their concrete outline, their deep-lying mystery—explain why
the great Europeans of the mind draw to themselves the
life and experience of successive generations, out of
which they grow richer every age by the harvests of the
preceding ages. *On ne prête qu'aux riches.* These four
figures, which Shakespeare, Cervantes, Tirso and Goethe
sculpted out of the dreams of the men of their days, grow
constantly out of the dreams of the days that follow; so
that, classic, they are always modern, and though clad in
the garb of the time in which they were born, they are
always up to date; and, born definitely English, Spanish,
German, they are always European, indeed universal,
with that specific branch of universality the European
spirit derives from its Socratic brain and from its
Christian heart.

2

HAMLET AND DON QUIXOTE*

FOR reasons that will become clearer as the pattern of
the two parallels is unfolded, Hamlet stands closer to
Don Quixote, while Faust is more in line with Don Juan.
But, if we are to understand the pattern, it is best to
start with an adequate understanding of its four elements.
Now it is an unfortunate fact that Hamlet, Prince of Denmark, naturalized English by Shakespeare, is just as apt to
be misunderstood by readers and audiences as he was by
his mother, by his uncle, by Ophelia and by the whole
Danish Court, not excluding Horatio. This situation
must have been deliberately created by Shakespeare, for
he was a conscious artist and knew what he was about. Be
that as it may, however, the fact is that even in our day,
leaving aside such fanciful and extravagant interpreta-
tions as the Freudian, an experienced and in many ways
great actor can still describe Hamlet as the man who
could not make up his mind. Lucky for the great actor
in question that the King of England of those days was
soft-headed enough to comply with the instructions conveyed in the spurious letter from Claudius (drafted and
forged by the man who "could not make up his mind"),
and so put to death Rosencrantz and Guildenstern; for,

*This parallel has been previously discussed, out of its present
context, in On Hamlet and in Spain.

otherwise Hamlet's two schoolmates might have had some curious comments to make on this alleged inability to make up his mind on the part of a man who so cavalierly had made up his mind to send them to their doom. Lucky again that the envious sliver broke and that, before it did, Ophelia's own mind had also broken; for otherwise Ophelia might also have commented on how the Prince who could not make up his mind resolved to break his promise of marriage and sent her for cold comfort to a nunnery. And again—but won't that do?

No. Hamlet suffered from no constitutional indecision whatsoever; nor was he too intellectual to act; nor was he effete nor, least of all, effeminate. Hamlet was a virile character, capable of swift decision whenever the motives thereto were compelling enough *for him*. This is forcibly illustrated by the contrast between his resolution in following the Ghost to the edge of the precipice and his hesitations and procrastinations about satisfying the Ghost's thirst for revenge.

Two factors are at play here: one is the social pressure round Hamlet; the other is the reaction against that pressure on the part of Hamlet. The social pressure is suggested by Shakespeare in the great second scene, when Hamlet, standing about and apart from all the Court, is yet the centre of all attention. It is explicitly described in Ophelia's lamentations, at the end of the "Nunnery" scene, and, particularly, in the famous three lines:

> The expectancy and rose of the fair State,
> The glass of fashion and the mould of form,
> The observed of all observers . . .

May I be allowed to say that these are perhaps the most

English lines in the play? They express, as only Shake-speare can express things, the social sense of the English to which they owe both their superb achievements as a nation and their "spleen", "melancholy", "boredom", and occasional freakness as individuals; the group-pressure which on the one hand makes one feel that every Englishman *is* the whole of England, and on the other makes every Englishman now and then, in his weaker moments, wish that it were not so. That is what Ophelia expresses, superlatively, because Hamlet is no ordinary citizen but the Prince. He is the expectancy of the fair State because he must act as he is expected; the glass of fashion, because he must lead close enough to the led not to lose touch with them; the mould of form, because he must limit himself to such forms as are ad-mitted by conformity; the observed of all observers because the "fair State", that is, the group, keeps its pressure relentlessly on all its members, but especially on the Prince.

In a man of no personal views, this situation might have led to comedy, rather than to tragedy. *Hamlet* is a tragedy because the Prince happens to possess personal ways. Shakespeare suggests it from the first also in the great second scene in the way he pits him out against the general conformity of the Court; as well as in a number of subtler details; but more especially, in Hamlet's own comment on the King's drinking.

> And as he drains his draughts of Rhenish down
> The kettle-drum and trumpet thus bray out
> The triumph of his pledge,

says Hamlet, and Horatio asks, "Is it a custom?" Horatio

had been studying at Wittenberg, so we swallow with less difficulty than we otherwise should, that a Dane should ask another Dane whether a custom of Denmark is a custom of Denmark. This shows that Shakespeare needed this question to be put for some purpose—which is no other than to express Hamlet's disconformity, *i.e.*, his refusal to be the mould of form, since he had substance of his own which would not go into the forms "the general" would accept. So, he answers:

> Ay, marry, is't.
> But to my mind, though I am native here
> And to the manner born, it is a custom
> More honour'd in the breach than the observance.

Note that "though I am native here". Hamlet himself emphasizes the opposition between his ways and the general way.

The potential forces, ready to enter into play, are now defined. On the one hand, a society conscious of itself exerting pressure on its prince; on the other, a prince conscious of that pressure but on the defensive against it in order to safeguard his own ways.

At this stage, the Ghost. It is not perhaps in Shakespeare's intentions, but it is in the nature of things that the burden of avenging his father should be laid on the unwilling shoulders of Hamlet by a ghost; for a ghost is a dead man coming from the past to lay down the law on the present; a ghost is, therefore, an excellent symbol for tradition. A society is, up to a point, governed by its dead, whom, in so far as they still prompt the living, we are entitled to visualize as ghosts. The Ghost of King Hamlet calls on the prince to avenge his murder as a

matter of course not to be called into question: the
pattern stands out clear, and those words of Hamlet,
"more honour'd in the breach than the observance,"
otherwise an irrelevant comment, acquire a sense and
a significance.   Hamlet is henceforth to struggle
between the social pressure of a tradition which
commands him to avenge his father, and his own
rebellion against the burden laid on him.

I have elsewhere analysed the deeper motive for
Hamlet's opposition and subconscious rebellion against
the traditional law; and shall not go into that aspect of
the matter here, since our present theme, Hamlet's
parallel with Don Quixote, does not require it. For our
present purpose, all we need note is that Hamlet is a man
of action at the centre and apex of a conscious society,
who is aware of a social pressure and a tradition against
which he is generally on the defensive, and, specifically
in what concerns his father's vengeance in a state of subconscious revolt.

Now Don Quixote is the very symmetry of all this.
He is an hidalgo lost in the plain of La Mancha, in a small
village, with nothing to do; no company but that of the
priest and the barber; no observers to observe him. He
is no man of action though he is fond of the chase; but
rather a dreamer, and an introverted one, as Cervantes
with his quiet humour conveys, saying: "In a village
close by there lived a farmer's daughter with whom
once upon a time he had been in love, though it is
understood that she never knew or realized it." This
idle dreamer, surrounded by a social void, had to
create his own society; and, in search of the raw
materials thereto, he went to the Books of Chivalry.
By dint of reading these fantastic tales, he came to

believe in them, or, in other words, he inserted himself into the imaginary society of the Books of Chivalry, for lack of a real society, to put enough pressure on him for his inner balance between his individual and his social self. Thus, instead of being a prince at the centre of a dense society, bearing the maximum of social pressure and observed by all observers, Don Quixote is an isolated man at the periphery of a rarefied society, unobserved by man or dog, with time and energy on his hands and nothing to do with them. Naturally enough, Hamlet seeks freedom from his society and Don Quixote seeks a society for his freedom.

Ophelia and Dulcinea symbolize these two attitudes; Hamlet shakes Ophelia off brutally, as soon as he perceives where the social pressure she incarnates is leading him. His visit to her in her closet, his "perusal" of her face "as he would draw it" admirably convey the distrust of the, as yet, free man for the woman who is on the eve of enslaving him to society; and the almost unbearably rough and cruel "nunnery" scene, the natural outcome and conclusion of the closet scene, achieves the rejection of the social chains by the rebellious prince: "I say we will have no more marriages. To a nunnery, go." Freedom from society.

Meanwhile, Don Quixote seeks society for his freedom. There is no woman in his life; so, on the slender basis of a youthful memory, the farmer's daughter Aldonza Lorenzo, whom he once vaguely and silently had loved in his youth, he builds up a lady, Dulcinea del Toboso, for whose love he will commit the most comic follies and the most tragic and heroic mistakes. Don Quixote surrendering his freedom without reserve, up to the death, to a woman almost of his invention is thirsting for social thraldom in a world without social pressure, just as Hamlet, rejecting Ophelia to a nunnery, is thirsting for freedom from social thraldom in a society too rich in social pressure. While Hamlet wanders about meeting at random with players, Norwegian captains and cemetery clowns, who time and again make him undergo the impact of that society he is shunning, Don Quixote goes out deliberately to meet a society that will not come to him, and if need be to invent it and to impress on it the stamp of his own inner world.

There is a moving symmetry between the soliloquies of Hamlet and the sallies of Don Quixote. The soliloquies are inner adventures, sallies of the man of action driven to passion by social pressure, and forced to explore his secret self; and they drive ever inwards like ingoing spirals to end in the point of a self-murderous bodkin; while Don Quixote's sallies and adventures are like soliloquies of the man of passion drawn out to action by the social void, and develop like outgoing spirals, till they are lost in the dust of the desert.

Hamlet and Don Quixote are thus the two European symbols for the most European of problems: that of the balance between individual man and social man. Hamlet incarnates the tortured soul of the men born free who have to live in a community too strong and too exacting for them; Don Quixote incarnates the equally tortured soul of the men born social who have to live in a community too loose and rarefied for them. The true European spirit would require such a political and social environment as would prevent any of us from becoming either a Don Quixote or a Hamlet. For the time being the trend points towards a world of Hamlets. Don Quixote is on the decline.

3

FAUST AND DON JUAN

WHEN from a comparative study of Hamlet and Don Quixote, we pass to that of Faust and Don Juan, the whole frame of reference seems to change along with the characters considered. Hamlet and Don Quixote have been suggesting to us tensions and problems of our daily life; and, in the end, have remained in our minds as two conjugated symbols of the adjustment or maladjustment between the individual and society. Faust and Don Juan, on the other hand, call forth problems of a religious rather than of a social import. This does not mean that religion is absent from the world of Hamlet and of Don Quixote; for nothing born in the sixteenth century ever could be conceived without religion; but it does mean that in the world of the Danish Prince and of the Spanish hidalgo religion is taken for granted and figures as one of the elements of life, and no more. In the world of Faust and of Don Juan, however, the question of the existence and of the essence of God is crucial; and according to whether God exists or not, and to whether He is understood in one way or another, the definition and the destinies of the two characters will have to change.

This explains perhaps the curious contrast between the respective literary histories of the two pairs of characters. Hamlet and Don Quixote are born once for all from Shakespeare and Cervantes. True they undergo a fresh interpretation as age follows age; but they remain in the history of European letters what their respective creators decided they should be. Faust and Don Juan, launched into the European Olympus by Marlowe and by Tirso de Molina within one generation of each other, are taken up again by other poets in later times and altered in their very core as the attitude towards religious matters changes in the interval. For, while Hamlet and Don Quixote are so to speak *horizontal* characters, types of manhood whose tensions and relations move sideways towards other men, Faust and Don Juan are *vertical* characters whose chief tensions are in the realm of absolute values—life, death, destiny, God.

Such is the underlying link between Faust and Don Juan who, otherwise, are opposite characters. The old and disillusioned German student, amidst his books and phials, longs for life; the youthful Spanish aristocrat, brimful of life and bent on enjoying it, has no thought for books and phials; indeed, no thought for anything. This contrast, by its very opposition, establishes also a relationship between the two. *In the limited sense in which they are here considered*, just as Hamlet is the anti-Don Quixote, and vice-versa, so Faust is the anti-Don Juan, and vice-versa. Faust is sense without sex; Don Juan is sex without sense. Or, in the terms of our European nomenclature, Faust is mind without will; Don Juan is will without mind.

It is now clear that just as Hamlet and Don Quixote symbolize the two possible failures of one European ideal —the happy balance of man in society—Faust and Don Juan symbolize the two aspects whose harmony is required for another European ideal—that of the intelligent impulse and that of the purposeful intellect. For strictly speaking will without mind is no longer will, but mere impulse; mind without will is no longer mind but mere intellect. Hence, by the way, a disparity between the attitude of Don Juan and that of Faust: Faust seeks youth, because the intellect, being aware of itself, and therefore of its own insufficiency, seeks the impulse; but Don Juan does not seek age, because the impulse is unaware of itself, and just is. Faust seeks life, experience and a put-on youth because he has exhausted his science and finds himself in a spiritual void; while Don Juan goes out into the world of adventures out of sheer fullness of inner vigour, not seeking to consume life, but to give it forth, or rather, seeking nothing, just giving life without thinking about it.

The two types appear in European literature in a similar way: shaped by their first poets out of a popular tradition. In the case of Faust, there was a fund of traditions and stories turning on the theme of the student who exploits his knowledge for personal selfish ends, a theme which leads to black magic and witchcraft. In the case of Don Juan, the figure rises out of a number of stories and traditions on the subject of a rake who, having dared to defy a dead man, finds himself dragged to damnation by the ghost or statue of the defunct. This supernatural element which surrounds their birth as permanent figures of European lore grants to both Faust and Don Juan that transcendental dimension which both possess: in both cases there was much tradition at the basis of the story. Johann Faustus, the student of Heidelberg, born just before the discovery of America, acquired a reputation for magic powers in which both Melanchton and Luther seem to have believed. As for Don Juan Tenorio, he was a rake of Seville, who slew the Commander Ulloa the very night he had stolen his daughter; the authorities dared not punish him for fear of his family, and tradition in the city asserted that the Franciscan friars of the monastery where the Commander was buried, in order to rid the city of her criminal son, killed him secretly in the monastery and spread the rumour that the rash youth had come to the chapel and had insulted the statue over the sepulchre: whereupon the spirit of the Commander had animated the statue and dragged Don Juan to Hell.

Such are the popular traditions on which Marlowe and Tirso de Molina created characters, which, after a varied literary evolution, are radically transformed in the early nineteenth century by Goethe and by Zorrilla. Marlowe endows the character with wonderful vigour. His Faust is clearly drawn from the outset on the basis of self-seeking and appetite. It is a selfish desire to enjoy pleasure and power that tempts him to conclude a covenant with the Devil:

> Oh what a world of profit and delight,
> Of power of honour, of omnipotence
> Is promised to the studious artizan!

Mephistopheles, as an honest devil's agent that he is (for honesty is essential to the tactics of trade even when the trade is dishonest in its strategy), delivers Helen to him, and so, Faust cries out his joy in lines in which the anxiety for his soul bursts through the exultation of his bliss:

> Sweet Helen, make me immortal in a kiss.
> Her lips suck up my soul. See where it flies!
> Come, Helen, come, give me my soul again.
> Here will I dwell, for heaven is in thy lips.
> And all is dross that is not Helena.

The catch is, of course (as in Stock Exchange transactions), in the time for settlement; when the fatal hour tolls, Faust must surrender his soul. He is honest, and he pays. And when Lucifer has secured his prey, the chorus comments in lines from which we gather the doctrine underlying the character and the whole play:

> Faustus is gone: regard his hellish fall,
> Whose fiendful fortune may exhort the wise
> Only to wonder at unlawful things,
> Whose deepness doth entice such forward wits
> To practise more than heavenly power permits.

This doctrine is clear. Man must not enquire into such things as Heaven put beyond the bounds of his intelligence. Wonder he may; enquire he must not. The penalty for transgression paid by the "forward wits" is damnation eternal.

Tirso de Molina is, at his best, as great a dramatist as Lope de Vega or Calderón. His *Burlador de Sevilla y Convidado de Piedra*, or "The Deceiver of Seville and Guest of Stone," is not his best play; but it has many an original feature, and, in particular, an effective use of what we might nowadays describe as literary *Leitmotive*. Chief of these *Leitmotive* is the flippant line Don Juan often flings back to those who remind him of the punishment that awaits him in the other life as a retaliation for his many sins in this. The carefree young man answers:

> Qué largo me lo fiáis!
> What long credit you grant me!

This gift for poetry and vigorous utterance typical of Tirso de Molina, serves his purpose admirably in this case; for the character appears from the first scene in all his energetic if impulsive activity. The play begins in the dark, in the hall of the palace of the King of Naples. Don Juan and Isabella, the young duchess he has infamously betrayed, come out of a room hand-in-hand, and the King himself, hearing the noise in the night, comes out also and asks, "Who is there?" The vigour of the answer in its original Spanish cannot be translated, though it comes entirely from its utter simplicity:

> — ¿Quién ha de ser?
> Un hombre y una mujer.

> — Who could it be?
> A man and a woman.

There, in a bold, discarnate sentence, is the essence of the play. In later scenes, similar passages abound, drawing, in vigorous strokes, the portrait of this ruthless, unruly egotist whose progress through life tramples all rules and persons indifferently. Saved from the ocean by a fisherwoman, he betrays her also, and in the love-making that goes to this betrayal, Tirso skilfully intertwines another of his *Leitmotive*. Flattered and hit by his words of love the fisherwoman, nevertheless, keeps saying:

> Quiera Dios que no mintáis,
> May God wish you do not lie,

the reiteration of which lends a delightful music to the

verse and an undercurrent of pathetic mistrust to her surrender.

After a chain of adventures swiftly disposed of by the dramatist, Don Juan comes to the strange doom to which the play owed much of its popularity. He happens to pass by the sepulchre of the Commander whom he had killed after having betrayed his daughter, and jestingly asks him to dinner. The stone statue of the dead man turns up at the appointed hour, seizes hold of his guest and drags him to Hell.

This melodramatic end was bound to draw the crowds in every nation. But there are other reasons for the universal success of Don Juan; one of which was that, being a woman-killer, he instantly became the idol of the fair sex all over Europe; for if he dealt with women infamously, he at any rate devoted his life to them, which is more than most men are willing to do. As Byron was to say, precisely in his *Don Juan*:

> Man's love is of man's life a thing apart,
> 'Tis woman's whole existence.

This state of affairs has, of course, changed a good deal since Byron's days, whether very deeply and for the better is another matter and for another occasion; but in the time that elapsed between the first and the last Don Juan, Byron's dictum held undisputed sway; and the fact undoubtedly contributed to the universal popularity and fascination of the type. There is perhaps at play a deeper reason as well: the two centuries during which Don Juan grows in popularity are precisely those in which Europe consolidates the modern State and society, with its imposing body of positive laws and of

religious and moral tenets. Don Juan swept throughout
Europe like a gust of anarchy blowing across the too well
groomed parks of Church and palace; an escape for the
European imagination from the tight hold of so many
laws.

Don Juan underwent in European literature more incarnations than any other character of man's creation.
He was first taken over by the Italians, who made him
shallower, in order to let him move more easily in the
shifting surroundings of Italian Comedy. It seems, though
the matter is not certain, that it was from this Italianate
version that Molière took his Don Juan. The more is the
pity; for, though delightful in its Molièresque touches of
human insight—such as the peasant courtship—the
Festin de Pierre presents a Don Juan who by no
means contributes to enriching the character. This Don
Juan is an out and out atheist and praises hypocrisy: two
features which stray from the right path of the character's
evolution. Worse still, Molière gives him ideas, the very
thing a woman-killer would have no use for. It is rather
to this than to the Spanish family that Da Ponte's libretto
of *Don Giovanni* belongs—and so we can but lament that
the loveliest music ever written should be wasted on a
futile story.

Don Juan's adventures in England begin in 1676 with
Shadwell's *The Libertine*, and end—so far—with Bernard
Shaw's John Tanner. Naturally, the honours go to
Byron. Who but an idle English aristocrat would turn
Don Juan into a tourist? For a Spaniard, the poem is
marred by mistakes Byron, as a European, might have
taken the trouble to avoid; such as rhyming Sancho
"*Panca*" with Salamanca, and Don Juan with ruin: and
calling a Spanish ship *The Most Holy Trinidada* which is

E

simply illiterate. For the character itself there is too
much Byron in it to salvage the chief feature which
makes the character of Don Juan what it is—its transcendental dimension.

Thanks to this feature, which in the Spanish tradition
he never lost, Don Juan, like Faust, changes radically at
the beginning of the XIXth century. In the case of Faust,
the change is due to Goethe. In his hands, Faust is no
longer the orthodoxy-bound mind who looks through
the walls of his dictated science moved by a sinful curiosity; but on the contrary, a *savant* who, having exhausted all earthly studies and found no satisfaction in
them, turns to a higher knowledge in the hope of light.
The perspective has been turned upside down. Marlowe's
Faust lived inside a pyramid of divine light emanating
from the apex of revelation; and out of which he must
not stray. Goethe's Faust lives in a world of diffused
light shining here and there in nature, and from the
observation of which men have to discover, if they can,
the hidden Source of Light. This Faust could not be
sentenced to eternal damnation if in his search for truth
he strayed into error; for in Goethe's day, error was no
longer an impudent challenge to revealed truth, but a
step towards a truth that lay somewhere further afield.
This Faust could only be punished if he happened to fall
into the other sin of Marlowe's Faust: that of seeking
truth for his own selfish lusts—power, glory, enjoyment.
And as soon as Goethe makes his Faust love the golden
instant for its own sake, he is saved.

Don Juan goes through exactly the same transformation about one generation later. Zorrilla, as a poet, was
to Goethe what Don Juan is to Faust. By a kind of poetical
instinct, he brought about in the Don Juan he found in

Tirso a change of perspective similar to that which
Goethe's thought had brought about in Marlowe's
Faust. He was the first to wonder what would happen to
Don Juan if he met with a wholly innocent maid who gave
herself to him out of pure love and without his having to
set in motion his arsenal of tricks. The outcome was a
play in two parts—again a curious parallel with Goethe's
Faust—in which the first is devoted to the usual outline
of Don Juan as a rake and the second to the experience
that is to save him. But with consummate skill, Zorrilla
"plants" this salvation in the boldest way at the end of
the first part. Don Juan has abducted Doña Inés from the
convent where she lived in innocence. She is in his
country home on the outskirts of Seville. She declares
her love for him. He discovers love. He is touched by a
kind of grace. Her father, the Commander, arrives on
the heels of one of Don Juan's rivals, Don Luis, whose
fiancée Don Juan had betrayed. Begging Don Luis to
stand by, Juan throws himself at the Commander's feet
and offers him fortune, life, obedience for the privilege
of being loved and perhaps saved by his daughter. The
old man indignantly spurns him and both he and Don
Luis treat the convert as a coward. Then Don Juan returns to his first self and cries out:

> I called to Heaven—in vain.
> Since its gates it closed on me,
> For my deeds on earth again
> Let Heaven answer. Not me.

This done he kills the two men and escapes as the gover-
nor's soldiers arrive on the spot.
    It is at this moment that Zorrilla asserts the rights of

56 THE EUROPEAN OLYMPUS

absolute love in a bold line, the very last of the first part.
One of the soldiers, on seeing the body of Doña Inés'
father, says: "Justice must be done to Doña Inés";
whereupon Doña Inés retorts: "Yes. But not against
Don Juan." The woman who thus dares screen with her
love the man who has just killed her father must satisfy
the audience that her love is such as to justify this exorbi-
tant claim. Doña Inés does. When the second part
begins, Don Juan, after a long absence, is beholding a
mausoleum which, by order of his father now dead, has
been erected to his victims. Among the sepulchres, he
sees one of Doña Inés. The statue of the dead maid
suddenly vanishes and her spirit speaks: she has asked the
Lord to take her soul for his, and the Lord has granted
that they should be saved or damned together. So that
now her salvation is in his hands. The revelation moves
him and when his boon-companions turn up, they mistake his emotion for fear at the macabre surroundings,
and laugh at him. To have his own back, he invites them
to dinner with the statue of the Commander; a detail,
by the way, which for the first time gives some sense to
this invitation. They accept; and when the statue turns
up, the friends, believing themselves hoaxed, challenge
him and kill him. Unaware of his own death, Don Juan
finds himself dragged by the Commander to Hell, when
with a last thought for Doña Inés he falls on his knees and
asks God to be forgiven. Doña Inés then extends a hand
from Heaven and saves him. Love has triumphed.

The two characters have undergone a similar transformation: Faust passes from selfish knowledge and damnation in Marlowe to self-giving love and salvation in
Goethe; Don Juan passes from selfish sex and damnation
in Tirso to self-giving love and salvation in Zorrilla.

Both the mind and the will of Europe change their polarity between 1600 and 1900; from "dare not or you shall be damned" to "dare and you will be saved—if your daring is pure". And the anxiety of our day is whether we are not drifting again to an era of "dare not or you shall be damned"—an era of black-magic and stone-guests that drag their hosts to Hell.

4

EUROPEAN SYMBOLS

JUST as Hamlet and Don Quixote can be considered as the symbols of the Englishman and the Spaniard, Faust and Don Juan, in a number of ways incarnate the German and the Spaniard. For the Englishman, like Hamlet, is a man of action hemmed in by a society very much aware of itself, watchful of its standards, alive to its traditions— a society in which many ghosts stalk the ramparts and speak with a commanding tone, and whose leading men are observed by all observers and must act as expected. While the Spaniard, like Don Quixote, is a man of passion living in a rarefied society, impatient of all traditions, rules or institutions, whose life is therefore a solitary walk in the desert, which he is free to people with his own imaginings. And the German, like Faust, is a lazy-willed but mentally active creature, skilful with dead materials but awkward with human beings, easily tempted by the selfish joy of power, ready to follow the devil without qualms should the Devil deliver him the object of his desire, and apt to prefer *Nordische List*, nordic craftiness, to a straight fight with his adversary; yet fond of ideas and ideals as one is fond of a blue sky while eating ham at a picnic. And, like Don Juan, the Spaniard is an anarchist, for whom all rules, human and divine, are but irksome shackles, quite capable of seeing to his own affairs without help of any Devil other than his own familiar one. This fidelity of the four types to three great European characters is already one of the ways in which their symbolic value for mankind is incalculable.

But there are others. The balance between society and the individual, a typically European problem, has been shown to be dramatically illustrated by Hamlet and Don Quixote. Faust and Don Juan incarnate two other con-jugated European moods. Faust stands for the spirit of enquiry. He incarnates that higher rationalism, that faith in the inner light of the human spirit which from the days of Socrates has led Europe to the discovery of science, of the planet and of the inner continents of man. Don Juan incarnates the spirit of expansion, discovery and conquest, which has made Europe the creator of America and the leader of world culture in the five seas. True, from Don Juan flow the crimes and follies which have stained the history of colonization and empire; as from Faust the errors, struggles and wars which the mental adventures of man have raised and are still raising around us; but in the case of both, the balance is positive and, as in the two later incarnations of the character, they are saved.

Finally, Faust and Don Juan are again European as symbols respectively of the social, mental, conscious, and of the individual, vital, subconscious powers of the spirit of Europe. For Faust is the incarnation of the rules and principles which regulate collective life; a scion of an aprioristic people, who like to think out beforehand the reasons why they must act—an attitude which often leads to *scheming* action; and, socially, to tyranny by over-legislation and an excess of foresight; leading in its turn to obedience to all the laws, even the bad ones, only because they have been thought out by those who ought to know. While Don Juan is the incarnation of absolute liberty, the scion of a people fond of acting first, and justifying itself afterwards, an attitude which leads to contempt for all laws, even the good ones; but on the other hand, a people fond of asserting the right of the individual soul to ultimate salvation, beyond and above any claims of society, of morality or of the law; saved, as the poet makes Doña Inés say, by the grace of a mystery beyond the ken of man. Don Quixote and Hamlet are neither saved nor damned. They are doomed to wander for ever among men, in the midst of their contemporaries, ever unsolved. But Faust and Don Juan, whose yearning is upwards, are saved—by woman.

> Das Ewigweibliche
> Zieht uns hinan.

Which can have no other meaning than that man is saved if and when and by what he creates in the ever-feminine womb of Time.

PART III

EUROPEAN TENSIONS

the case of the Spaniards. The Germans feel in touch
with their source through the continuous flow of the
river of their collective life; the Spaniards, every one
of them, separately, feels the beginning of things in the
native and pristine impetus of fire that rises in him.

This contrast between an original sense flowing from
the past and an original impulse rising from below is
manifest in the two languages. German is, of all the chief
languages of Europe, the one in which the letter *U*
is most frequent. Then the English prens *it* is *m*
in German; and the English suffix *ing* is *ung* in German.
U is the original vowel *par excellence*. The original
sense of things has in no language a more adequate
expression than the German prefix *Ur*. The physical suggestion conveyed by the prefix *Un* is typical of the fluid
nature of German thought. The length and weight of the
words adds to the impression; and the manner of handling separate particles of verbs, leaving them for the end
of the phrase, sometimes a very long one, shows that
that German thought can remain fluid and in suspense
for a longer time than that of any other European.

This weight of the German language comes from the
predominance of consonants over vowels; perhaps the
highest in European languages, certainly so if only the
chief of these languages are considered. Here, again,
German and Spanish stand poles apart, for Spanish is
perhaps the richest in vowels of all the languages of
Europe, thus suggesting the gaseous character of fire.
By "richest in vowels" is here meant the feature exactly
opposite of that just observed in German, the predominance of vowels over consonants in any given page.
There is another sense in which the phrase could hardly

1

THE THREE LATIN SISTERS

THERE is a Spanish doggerel curiously applicable to France, Italy and Spain:

> Tres eran tres,
> Las hijas de Elena,
> Tres eran tres;
> Y ninguna era buena.[1]

Daughters of Helen, for the three Latin Sisters are, through Rome, the heirs of Greece; and as for none of them being good, that, of course, goes without saying. "Not-good" is a concept implied in the verb "to be"; so we should not worry too much about that. But the point in the doggerel is that none of the three need give herself airs or look down on the two.

This point was worth making; for the three Latin Sisters are very touchy on matters of precedence. Indeed, it may well be that the hardest core of the tensions between them is due precisely to that subtle kind of precedence known as prestige (a word, by the way, the English had to import from France). Such matters only

---

[1] Three they were, three—the daughters of Helen—Three they were, three—And none was good.

arise among equals or near-equals. But equal here does not mean "the same" nor even "alike".

Though they have been grouped here together under the common epithet "Latin", it does not follow that France, Italy and Spain are particularly alike. On the contrary: what strikes the observer is not how alike but how unlike they are despite their common Roman heritage. The richest part of this heritage was a common language. How different the three "Latin" Sisters must be is shown by their capacity to evolve from this same stock three languages as different as French, Italian and Spanish. More on this anon, when, as in other later cases, due weight will be given to the differences between the three languages in order to value the differences between the national characters which they express.

Their common origin, however, does set up among the three Latin sisters a "resonance" of the kind described in a later part of this book. The three derive from Rome a sense of the State as an authority from above, a sense wholly alien, for instance, to the tradition of Britain, where the State (until in recent times Britain fell into socialist ways) always was a growth from below, a true democracy in the pure and original sense of that much debased word. This Roman background shared by France, Italy and Spain does provide the three peoples with a common idiom, a common subconscious attitude, which amounts to a political and sociological family likeness. It is from this point of view, if not from others, that the description "Three Latin Sisters" is justified.

But sisters do not always live in the best possible relations; and the Three Latin Sisters are apt to differ and to allow between them psychological tensions which add much zest and liveliness to European affairs.

A. FRANCE—ITALY

The Franco-Italian tension is by no means one of the strongest in Europe; but it is definite enough to provide a model for, and an introduction to, the study of more complicated cases. It is more eager and active at the Italian end, where it is apt to adopt acute intellectual forms, clever arguments, elaborate explanations. These, however, are but the foliage of the tree. Hidden under the earth is the root of the trouble: *Envy*.

Strange, is it not? There is no reason whatever why Italy should be envious of France or of any other nation, for the Italian people are one of the most gifted in the world. And, to be sure, no trace of envy, of France or of anybody, can be found in Italy until she became a nation, in 1870. Then it was that Italy, as a political power, began to feel envious of France as a political power. The argument (for there are arguments also in the realm of feelings) would seem to run: "We are as creative a people as the French; therefore we ought to be a nation as powerful as France." The fault in the argument is obvious: the fact that the Italians are as rich in creative qualities as the French does not prove that they can vie with the French in political and other collective talents. Historical events are by no means the fanciful blossomings of a capricious fate. They are in nature and follow its laws. We do not expect pears from apple trees nor apples from pear trees. The fact that Italy did not achieve its unity till nearly the end of the nineteenth century while France was a strong State four centuries earlier, is not fortuitous. The influence of the Vatican as an obstacle to the growth of an Italian State is evident. But when all allowances are made for this fact, enough remains to warrant the conclusion that the difference between the political evolution of France and that of Italy was mostly due to the action of natural laws operating through the character of the two peoples concerned.

It may well be that the deepest motive of this rivalry which Italy feels towards France comes from the core of that common Roman tradition mentioned above (also observable, though in a different context, in the rivalry between France and Spain). This common tradition perpetuates the sense of world unity which animated the Roman Empire and which, in a different light, manifests itself also in the Vatican. In actual practice, so far as Italy is concerned, it polarises itself towards the leadership of the Latin world, which to a considerable extent, means "Latin"-America. Observe how this "Latin" is smuggled into America from every corner of the earth which for some reason or other finds it convenient to oust Spain from the Continent she discovered. Had Spain held in the technical era the power and prestige which she conquered for herself in the religious era, the other two Latin sister countries might have maintained better relations. But when Spain fell from the apex of world power, France, who had played an important part in the events that brought about this downfall, made a bid to replace Spain as the leading nation of the Latin world. Italy was not then in a position to claim a share in the Spanish spoils, for she had not even attained her unity as a nation. Yet, in her national consciousness, there lived two powerful traditions which made her feel Rome as the centre of the world. Rome had been the mother and queen of the Roman Empire; Rome was—and is—the dome of the Catholic Church. Where could such a centre of history be found in the whole world?

What city could lay such claims to lead the whole world, and therefore, at any rate, the Latin world?

Yet the Italians had to admit that the Latin world, unconvinced by these historical appeals, was inclined to consider as its capital, not Rome but Paris. Whether the Latin world was right or wrong matters but little to our purposes and would be moreover as idle as difficult to discuss. The fact remains that if there is such a thing as a leadership of the Latin world—which is doubtful—it is to be sought, not in Italy but in France.

The moment has not yet come to discuss the position of Spain in this respect, but this much must be said: that the sources of Spain's influence over the Latin world have little or nothing to do with "leadership," for they are hidden in the subconscious being of Spain and of the Spanish-American countries. This circumstance, however, makes but stronger and sharper the competition between France and Italy, for this competition is circumscribed to the realm of the intellect.

It so happens that both France and Italy are rich in intellectual gifts. Both have brought invaluable contributions to the common fund of European culture. It also happens that these contributions belong to almost identical sectors of the spirit. France and Italy are the two mothers of form. They have provided Europe with the framework, the rules, the norms of its culture. While Spain, England, Germany and later Russia created the characters of European life—Don Quixote, Don Juan, Hamlet, Faust, Ivan Karamazov—Italy and France built the stage on which these characters stood and moved. This likeness in their creative gifts dooms France and Italy to constant strife.

Based on similarity in essentials, their rivalry is

further stimulated by difference in detail. France tends
to equilibrium and seeks measure in all things. This
feature of the French character may be connected with
the prevalence of the letter *E* (representing the sound as
in *bed*) in the French language. The full round vowels
of the Latin language are flattened out by French into
E. *Pater, mater* become *père, mère*. The predominance of
the letter *I* (pronounced EE) in Italian is even stronger
than that of *E* in French. I do not know whether anyone
has ever undertaken a statistical study of the recurrence
of particular vowels in the main languages of the world,
but I doubt whether it would be possible to find any
vowel more predominant in any language than *I* is in
Italian. Now, *I* is the most pointed vowel there is. Such
a pronounced preference for *I* must correspond to a
definite feature in the Italian character. It suggests a
persistent *intent* aiming pointedly at a sharply defined
target. It brings to mind the fact that the Italians excel
in the art of fencing. So do the French, of course, but
then we must expect to meet at every turn with this
likeness between the two Latin peoples. I have already
shown elsewhere how and why the French are specially
addicted to foreseeing, which again brings to mind that
much overworked French word : *Attention*. Now, attention and intent are close cousins. But under their family
air there is an important difference : attention looks on,
without pressure or motion; intent is animated with
both motion and pressure. While the French look at the
world with their intellect, the Italians drive into it the
point of an intent spirit.

Behind this intent we guess therefore a motive power,
a fire, a passion. A passion it had to be, which discrimi-
nates the Italians from the French, for the French are not

passionate. I have elsewhere[1] sketched a parallel explanation of the Frenchman and the Spaniard as respectively the man of thought and the man of passion. The Italian, therefore, incarnates a kind of synthesis of the Frenchman and of the Spaniard. The Italian is the only integral Latin: "Pathic" as the Spaniard, intellectual as the Frenchman. His passion is bound to work against the balance of pure intellection; which again explains the recurrence of the letter *I* in Italian. For we know that the frequency of *E* in French stands for measure and balance. And it is noteworthy (but far from unexpected) that while the Spaniard expresses the fullness of his passionate nature in the prevalence of the full vowels, *O* and *A*, the Italian passion has been sharpened by his keen intellect so that it expresses itself at the other extreme—not that of fullness but that of acuteness, not that of *O* and *A* but that of *I*.

This keen, steely foil of the Italian intellect pierces through the problem of Italo-French relations, and by the very power of its insight, whets the pain which these relations cause in the Italian soul. For the Italians, France has no claim to lead the Latin peoples. This conviction, contrasted with the success of France, sets up an inferiority complex in them. They have Rome, both the Latin and the Catholic, the twin suns of universality; and yet, it is France with her facile, obvious, superficial Place de l'Etoile, which is the centre of the world: by a kind of magic, France has caught the world in a web of words, ideas and luminous lines. At the centre of the web, the spider of French intellect, motionless but radiant. And from the south-east, the stiletto of Italian

[1] *Englishmen, Frenchmen, Spaniards.* Oxford University Press, London.

F

intention, like a sharp *l*, pointing at the spider.

The spider weaves on. For it is a notable feature of this Franco-Italian tension that France feels no antagonism whatever towards Italy in the political field—leaving aside, of course, phases and episodes—while in the cultural field, France is too intelligent not to feel the admiration which Italian genius commands. Even here, however, the gifts of the two nations are too akin for a profound influence to have exerted itself in either direction, despite the frequent wars the French carried into Italy at all times. True, the French learnt to write sonnets and comedies from the Italians; true, they followed in the steps of the great Italian artists who opened the era of modern art; but so did everybody else in Europe. In the mastery of great things—architecture and statesmanship, for instance—the French owe less to Italy than most other European nations.

All this may contribute to explain that curious inattentive way of the French towards the Italians. Paris thinks of London, of Berlin, even of Madrid more than it thinks of Rome.

B. FRANCE—SPAIN

The tension between France and Spain is mostly one between form and substance, or between talent and genius, or between woman and man. Not that France is effeminate. Far from it. (To be effeminate, moreover, one must be a man. Women are never effeminate.) But the spirit of France is feminine. Hence the tendency of so many of her artists to seek their inspiration in Spain. Corneille and Hugo stand out in their respective epochs as artists rich in form-giving, *i.e.*, feminine gifts, fecundated by masculine Spain. Ravel and Debussy, two characteristically feminine artists, are haunted by Spain. So are also Chabrier, Bizet, Lalo. Goya is the father of the French XIXth century in painting; Picasso the father of the XXth. The fascination of Spain continues to the present day with Montherlant and Camus in literature, Barraud in music.

This feminine spirit manifests itself in form. The Spaniard of all times and of all walks of life tends to seek form in France—and therefore to admire France for the perfection of her form. But the Spaniard is not susceptible to what is known as inferiority complex, mainly because he is too weak in collective sense to be afflicted by feelings based on collective reactions, such as those caused by nation or class. A particular Spaniard may admire France or the French as much as he wishes. It will always be as Mr. So and So, but never as a Spaniard, and therefore the national complex—whether of inferiority or of superiority—does not arise.

Moreover, the polarity between Spain and France from this point of view differs from a similar polarity, to be discussed later, between France and Germany, in that while Germany "flows", Spain "springs". Notice the strong prevalence of the *Sp* combination in all that pertains to Spain, beginning with the very name of the country. Thus, spontaneity is the characteristic feature of the Spaniard. Spring came to my pen of its own in connection with Spain and with that masculinity of the Spaniard which suggests yet another spontaneous gift of nature in its spring—sperm. The discontinuous, sporadic (Sp again), fitful and explosive character of Spanish life, its original strength, its vigour, irresistible but short-lived and as in spurts, its unco-operative nature, its incapacity to fall into shape, to weave itself into a continuity, to obey any norms, are strongly polarised with corresponding weaknesses and virtues of the French character. For the French, the Spaniard is lacking in measure. In French, Spanish words are apt to take on a pejorative sense, to suggest bombast and exaggeration. *Hablar* (to speak) gives *hableur* (braggart). Conversely, the Spaniard is apt to see French measure as meanness. It is worth noticing that the vowel *E*, the recurrence of which in the French language is (as I have explained elsewhere) the phonetic sign of measure and balance in the French character, should be in Spanish the phonetic sign of mean and ridiculous smallness. The normal diminutive for *viejo* (old man) is *viejecito*; but a ridiculous old man is *vejete*. This is general. The diminutive in *ete* suggests that which is small precisely in a ridiculous way. A *sombrerito* is just a little hat. A *sombrerete* is a ridiculous little hat.

A similar deliberate intention to deride mean, small ridiculous things by means of the letter *E*, precisely the symbol of measure in French, may be found in words such as *pequenene* (small man), *mequetrefe* (coxcomb), *pelele* (Jack Straw), and most telling of all, for it comes from the French, *petimetre*, a thoroughly ridiculous beau. The systematic, though of course quite subconscious character of the use of *E* to represent what one wishes to belittle is evident. It is aptly illustrated in the contrast between *vejete* and *viejito*, for, by all phonetic rules, the first syllable of these two words should be identical, yet the *i* is retained in *viejito* while it disappears in *vejete*, which clearly shows the non-phonetical, and therefore the psychological, origin of the difference. The fact is that the *i* is dropped in *vejete* because the language seeks to press down the word to a uniform row of *E*'s in order to drive home its deriding intention.

This contrast between the attitudes of the French and of the Spanish languages towards the sound *E* sheds a flood of light on the Franco-Spanish tension. It shows that what for the French is a virtue, measure, is for the Spaniard a vice, meanness. The Spaniard is apt to look upon the French as on a people who are always too much aware of unworthy details of life even in situations when a loftier and a more disinterested outlook should be required: money when death is at stake; wise tolerance when adultery has stained the honour of the male; and such like cases in which the Spaniard is absolute and acts regardless of consequences; and therefore he tends to look down on French relativity and foresight. This is a source of constant estrangement in the international relations between the two countries, for the French are good bargainers and efficient merchants of politics, while the Spaniard resents the bargaining spirit in matters of State. In fact the Spaniard sees the French as a nation inclined to avarice. Foresight is abhorrent to him, while it is the very stuff of the French soul.

This contrast follows from the masculinity of Spain and the femininity of France. Spain is a great hunger; France, a great fear. Spain is for adventure; France for security. Spain is for squandering; France for saving. Spain is extravagant like nature; France is sparing like art. When History turns against them, France spares herself and Spain devours herself.

But, of course, France *is* far more than Spain, for Frenchmen are mostly France; while Spain is mostly Spaniards. This again follows from our premises. The predominance of vertical over horizontal forces, *i.e.*, of nature manifesting itself directly and afresh every time in every Spaniard rather than of History and tradition continuing themselves all the time, is typical of Spanish life. This explains the weakness of Spain as a nation and the vigour and dourness of the Spaniard as a man. It explains also why hungry Spain has not devoured France.

Towards France, therefore, the attitude of the Spaniard is either the indifference of the man of the desert who knows neither France nor England, nor does he care; or else the admiration of the male for the female, of genius for talent, of substance for form. Spain can fecundate rather than create. It lacks that long patience which Buffon called genius—but then Buffon was a Frenchman and therefore had but little idea of what genius is at all, and he meant talent. A Spaniard has not got this long patience. The Frenchman is rich in it. The Spaniard admires him for it and openly, for he has no pride about it. Why should he be patient? He is content with what he is. "Pride"—said a French classic (I forget whether La Rochefoucauld or Montesquieu)— "pride prevents the Spaniard from working; vanity makes the Frenchman work." All this tallies. It is the female who works to shape what the male has fecundated. It is talent which shapes what genius has quickened. And while genius is proud, talent is vain.

In their turn, the French look upon Spain as a wild country. "Africa begins at the Pyrenees," wrote one of them. And since Louis XIV of France wrenched from the trembling hands of the ghostly Charles II of Spain the splendours of the Spanish imperial sun, Frenchmen have only too often endeavoured to belittle the historical and cultural achievements of Spain in order to assert the claims of France to Latin supremacy. Spain is not in a position to take up the challenge, for the strength of the Spanish spirit is not in Spain but in the Spaniard. And so her case goes by default. English text-books on the *Cid* of Corneille still uphold the untenable view that Corneille wrote a masterpiece out of a rough-hewn Spanish *comedia* of Guillén de Castro; though an objective examination shows that Corneille when writing his play was unable to shake off the sway of the manly Spanish poet over his mind.

Needless to say, much of this endeavour aims at fascinating Spanish America. It was the French who invented the name "Latin"-America, which the Anglo-Saxons later found so convenient in order to elbow Spain out of the world she had discovered. The XIXth century was favourable to these tendencies. Spain was slowly rebuilding a new outlook for herself after the collapse of the Old Régime, and the Spanish-American nations were still vibrating with the memories of the wars of emancipation, still unable to see in these wars mere Spanish civil wars, all too true to pattern. French culture was the handiest, the neatest, the easiest to assimilate. In the XIXth century Spanish America became "Latin" America, and its culture, outwardly at any rate, became French. As late as 1935, when I visited Lima, the association of Peruvian culture which invited me to lecture there styled itself "Chez Nous", though by then, its chairman felt already a bit ridiculous about it.

Had Spain been another kind of nation, this attitude of France might have been resented as an intrusion, and might have led to friction. But there is a wondrous amount of indifference in the Spanish character, and particularly towards the simple, daily efforts of the ox of perseverance. What is an ox, anyhow, in the land of bulls? In fact, although in the world of letters, of culture and even of politics, France often took an attitude of rivalry rather than of co-operation, she has been for long, and still remains, the most popular of European nations in Spain. This was not always so. The first inrush of France into Spain on a big scale—the invasion of Napoleon—called forth a vigorous reaction on the part of the people; almost a holy war, so that to kill French-men in 1808–14 was almost as fine an action as to kill Moors had been in the Middle Ages. Only a handful of intellectuals preferred the dictatorship of Napoleon to the obscurantism of the Old Régime—they were stigmatized as *afrancesados*.

During the nineteenth century, however, the people veered over, if not to the position of the *afrancesados*, at least to the liberal principles which had prompted it. France became for liberals and democrats the Mecca of freedom and democracy, and the *Marseillaise* the real anthem of all "progressive" Spain. This did but increase the anti-French bias of traditionalist Spaniards, who were thus, rather absurdly, led to turn their sympathies to Germany.

This split in the very core of Spain explains her neutrality in European affairs. The very opposite of the neutrality of Switzerland, which is a unanimous national decision not to meddle in Europe, Spanish neutrality results from the cancelling out of two eager desires to enter the European lists on opposite sides.

C. ITALY—SPAIN

The relations between Spain and Italy, once so close,

have become rarer in modern times. In the old days it was frequent to see Italians in Spain, in the service of the King, or Spaniards in Italy as viceroys, generals, cardinals or ambassadors. In the wake of these high dignitaries, men of letters came and went—as the illustrious instances of Cervantes and Quevedo show. Thus was the Italo-Spanish tension established from the earliest days, predominantly as one between a subjugated people and its Spanish political masters, in Italy, and between a people wishing to learn and its Italian cultural masters, in Spain. Italy was for Spain the mistress of the arts. Spain was for Italy the source of armies and of imperial authority.

So much for the old tension, traces of which remain in its contemporary counterpart. But to-day, and in its living context, the tension is quite different, indeed, in some ways, its values have been reversed. Italy is to-day closer to the rank of a great power than Spain, and as a border case, has always been more jealous of the privileges of great powers than greater powers were. Italy was always in the front rank of the opposition against claims made by Spain in this connection—for instance in the League of Nations. There is always bound to be between Spain and Italy this subconscious desire of Italy to efface the memories of the days when she was to a great extent ruled by Spain. The tension is therefore sure to contain a certain element of more or less spontaneous, more or less worked-up contempt for the Spaniard.

Alongside of this feature, there is in the Italo-Spanish tension a certain element of confraternity born of an undoubted likeness. For when all is said and done, and there is a certain amount to be said on differences, the likeness is considerable. Climate and land have made of Spain and Italy two nations closely alike, often apt to look at things and to live in the same way. The blue sky, a glass of wine, a lovely face, an hour of leisure, are apt to call forth a similar light in the eye of both Italian and Spaniard. This works for mutual understanding and close connection. The reaction is the stronger when the likeness is found to be but a superficial feature at the mercy of stronger and deeper differences.

By and large, the Italian is an extravert and the Spaniard an introvert. This can be observed in the language. The Spanish word often drops as useless a certain amount of "drapery" which the Italian language retains. *Osservatore—observador.* The Italian enjoys and tastes his language, while the Spaniard just throws it at you. This reveals a deeper difference between the two peoples. The Italian is more conscious of living, he cultivates the arts of life more and better than the Spaniard. When we hear him, we perceive the relish with which he speaks, the snapping of the tongue and the smacking of the lips, as if every word were a *boccato di cardinale.* Moreover Italian is the subtler language of the two. Its sounds have more delicate shades and differences than can be perceived by the somewhat elementary Spanish ear. It is a silkier language, less colourful perhaps, certainly less vigorous, less bony and stony than Spanish, but one which reveals a more delicately tuned intellect and a more persevering and careful purpose.

All this suffices to explain a certain feeling of superiority in the Italian, which the memories of his past subjection to the Spanish "barbarians" tend further to enhance. But it does not follow that a corresponding feeling of inferiority sets in in Spain. The Spaniard, on the contrary, looks upon the Italian with amusement.

He finds the Italian overflowing and romantic, and is shocked at his lack of soberness. Moreover, the very likeness of the two languages tends to make each of them appear as the caricature of the other. "For Heaven's sake speak like everybody else"—the Spaniard who hears Italian spoken, or the Italian who hears Spanish spoken, feels like saying. Worse still, Italian is the language of opera; and this fact has disastrous effects on Italy's prestige in Spain. Why in Spain and nowhere else? Because the likeness of the two languages is so close that Italian sounds to the average Spaniard like a kind of fake Spanish which one uses only on the stage while one is wearing a wig and a tin dagger and has to go through all the motions of killing the villain in the play, but, of course, *tutto convenzionale*. In short, for the Spaniard, Italian does not sound true. Everything an Italian says to a Spaniard sounds as just stage-script, which is not meant to be true and is only said for the sake of the spectators. This is so much the case that there are Italian words which have passed into Spanish, but with a meaning strictly limited to the operatic world. *Elenco*— a list, any list in Italian—means in Spanish the list of the singers of an opera and cannot even be applied to the list of the actors of a comedy or a drama. *Argumento* means argument in a discussion, but also (under Italian influence) the subject of a play.

This curious detail leads the Spaniard to under- estimating the Italian in a way entirely unjustified; for in many walks of life, and particularly in technical matters, the Italian is entitled to the respect of any Spaniard. There are other features of the Italian character which also raise the tension between Italy and Spain: chief of which is that *intent* we have already met with when comparing the Italians and the French, a feature which is generally considered in Spain as lacking in dignity. "A noble bull" is a bull which attacks when provoked, but does not wait, intent to catch you unawares. In politics also it is considered despicable for a man to be intent and persevering in his parliamentary fights. He is expected to take on a challenge when it comes, to meet it and leave it behind. But that set purpose, that sharp intent of the prolonged and keen "*I*" is an unpleasant feature in the eye of the Spaniards.

The Spaniards have a long historical connection with the Italians, and throughout the XVIth century often fought alongside of them in the imperial army. From the days of Charles V, they learnt to put more trust on Spanish or German units than on Italian ones. It is one of the psychological curiosities of the Italian people, that though a brave people, it dislikes being drafted into regular units and fighting in formation. Magnificent pilots, horsemen, motorists, swordsmen, they dislike soldiering. This is perhaps the reason why Spaniards do not seem to attach a special importance to Italian claims to world—or even to Latin—leadership. There is perhaps another reason: Spain has been singularly fertile in arts and letters during the last two or three generations. Rightly or wrongly, she considers her record in this matter above that of Italy. And deep down in her subconscious being, Spain feels perhaps that nothing Italy may do in this field will ever dim what remains of the light of Spanish past glories. Yet, Italy has not said her last word, and the most creative work of Spain, that of Spanish America, threatened from the north by the Anglo-Saxon impulse, is perhaps threatened from the south also by Italian vitality.

2

FRANCE—GERMANY

THE tension between Germany and France, the strongest and most constant on the Continent, is the main feature of the psychological landscape of Europe. The split in Charlemagne's Empire marks the beginning of an age-long duel between the two branches of the Germanic community. This split was by no means a mere result of the division of the paternal estate between the sons of Charlemagne. It was mainly due to other historical causes or circumstances, chief among them, perhaps, the difference in mental and moral attitude, nay, in psychological make-up, between the two peoples on either side of the Rhine.

To the east, the Germans, a people whose way of living had been for long that of wandering tribes, and who therefore were apt to look on life as something ever in flux, never to be caught and shaped inside hard and fast moulds; a people in whose collective soul ideas and feelings constantly flow out of each other in ever rolling motion, like clouds in the sky which the wind drives on, leaving them no respite to stay their course and acquire a definite profile.

To the west, the French, a people always ready to shape its life into concrete and definite forms, so that even the most unimportant happenings of daily life possess their models and must adjust themselves to long-established precedents. With them, all seems intent in trapping the fleeting instant, so as to turn its living light into a coin or medal of clear and careful but hard and fast design.

This contrast between the dominant tendency in the German and that in the French turn of mind foredooms them to a constant tension, dangerous though fertile. The Franco-German duel manifests the opposition between molten metal and pre-shapen mould; between flowing river and concrete walls and dykes. Their sense of flow leads the Germans to constant change; their sense of form makes change abhorrent to the French. The Germans remain always in touch with the sources and origins of their ever-flowing life; the French, on the contrary, seem always to rest on the end of life, where there is no longer any more to say, to wish, to think, and above all to change. (Hence their polish, their *finish*.) And so the Germans seem always to remain Barbarians who are still at an early stage of their historical career, ready to "march" towards their future; while the French are like a people who have completed the process of their self-civilisation and have no other desire left but to sit down comfortably and tell stories for the sake less of the tale itself than of the way it is told.

An examination of the two languages will confirm these first impressions. The chief feature of the German language in this respect might well be the prevalence of the word WERDEN; that of the French language, the partitive article. The idea which *werden* expresses is represented in other European languages by verbs such as *become* in English or *devenir* in French, which though not rare in their respective languages are by no means omnipresent. In Spanish, there is no word whatever to express such an idea—a fact which deserves separate treatment. But in German, *werden* is the verb most frequently used, and it acquires a special importance as an auxiliary. A thing in German *is* not done; it *becomes* done. This feature imparts to the language a kind of continuous motion, a sense of flow. The qualities and states which the verbs convey are not fixed; they *are* not; they *become*. They do not stand; they move towards their next state, or rather stage, which will itself be but another becoming towards an ever fluid beyond. The German language, therefore, reduces to its barest minimum the instant we call the Present, merging it into the instants before and after. Hence the avoidance of *sein*, to be, which the German discards for *werden*, to become, precisely in order to express that sense of fluidity which is the deepest feature of the German life. The fact that this verb, specific in its meaning and limited in its use in other languages, has a general meaning and is omnipresent in Germany, permeates the whole German language and thought with this most fluid of ideas. What for England or France is but a thought among many, and for Spain even no thought at all, is for Germany the very essence of all thinking; so that both language and thought take on in Germany the fluidity of a stream.

The French language, on the other hand, presents a curious, typical feature which singles it out among the other European languages—the partitive article. First and foremost, the partitive article is an article characteristic of substances, *i.e.*, things that keep the same name when they are divided into *parts*. We say *de l'eau* because any part of water is as much water as the whole of the water there is. At the outset, we observe the abstract nature of this feature of the French language. In other languages words such as *water* present to the mind concrete objects which strike it with an immediate impact. The French partitive article, however, puts between the object and our mind an intellectual curtain or veil which prevents us from perceiving the object directly, and only allows through the idea of the object. *Water* is a concrete object of nature. *De l'eau* is an abstract concept, a form or a property of nature, an attribute of God—a quality one contemplates with the mind rather than a body one handles and touches.

Nor does the use of the partitive article cease here. The French language reveals a curious trend in favour of it, so that its field of uses tends to increase. One does not merely use it in such sayings as *de l'eau, de la pierre*; but in: *il fait de l'allemand*; *il fait de la philosophie*; and even *il fait de l'entérite*; *il fait de la tuberculose*. This is the outward, linguistic sign of the French tendency to see things and facts as abstractions. Thus it is that life, which for the Germans is like a river, is for the French like a string of clear cut crystals. Everything becomes, everything flows for the German. Everything for the French is limited by hard and fast planes and can only change by sudden re-crystallizations into equally set forms. And this contrast between their respective ways of seeing and feeling life is perhaps the main cause of the tension between the two peoples.

A number of consequential tensions follow. The barbaric German is in love with the final, perfected if not perfect, civilization of the French. There is no European the German loves and admires as he does the Frenchman. And with no trace of envy. Not that the

German is free from envy altogether. Far from it. We shall in due course come across German envy, but not in relation to France. The hatred, the scorn the Germans often evince towards the French are but the thorns of the rose of their love for France. They are so awkward, that they present their nosegay thorns outward. The formless flow is in love with the crystal, and its ever-moving stream feels a deep, never-satisfied longing for the fixed mirror of the French intellect. In its muddy bed, the German force streams furiously, conquered and daunted by the grace of France. Now and then it overflows and overruns the whole of France, like a powerful river with its slime-laden waters.

Nevertheless, this tension between German force and French grace is no duel between Caliban and Ariel. Such an interpretation would do scant justice to Germany without in any way showing France in her true colours either. For Caliban is nature's impulse without the spirit; and Germany is by no means lacking in spiritual force; while Ariel is the symbol of a lighter and more evasive spirit than that of France. Both France and Germany are rich in spirit, and, despite their differences, a spirit of a truly similar kind, indeed of the same essence, just as clouds and crystals of snow, despite their differences, are but forms of water.

It is perhaps to this underlying unity that the rich relationships are due that bridge over the differences between the two peoples. How does France correspond to the love Germany feels towards her? One thing is certain—France is not in love with Germany. But that is neither here nor there, since love does not come natural to France. Yet, if we leave aside love, of which there can be no question, France feels an earnest and substantial attachment towards Germany. It may even be said that, quite apart from military and political considerations, Germany is the nation that commands her main attention and regard. Chief among the feelings of France towards Germany is respect — a respect which springs less from a desire to honour and exalt Germany than from an objective estimate of the high value of certain German qualities. For, it so happens that the peculiar gifts of France make of her perhaps the aptest nation in Europe to appraise the spirit of Germany, while the differences in the respective characters of the two peoples act rather as a stimulus than as an obstacle to such a study. What France respects most in her eastern neighbour is her force—a natural consequence of all that goes before. No one then should wonder at the fact that even when her eastern wooer turns bullish and brutal, and invades and devastates her, France should still feel an underlying current of attraction towards the object of her detestation.

We may now try to disentangle the knots of mutual inferiority-complexes with which these two peoples have tied themselves together. The love Germany feels towards France is steeped in modesty and even in humility; while the respect France feels towards Germany rests on a sense of weakness and inferiority. Each of the two peoples admires and seeks in the other what it feels lacking or deficient in itself. But though the feelings are symmetrical, their consequences are not. The Germans, after long phases of admiration and courtship, suddenly turn brutal, overpower France and seek to master her; the French live in a permanent state of respect, reserve, a regret perhaps that better relations are not possible, a state which, after their intellectualistic nature, they rationalize and endeavour to make reasonable.

Hence one at any rate of the roots of the war-like spirit of Germany and of the French pacifism, as they appear now, in their true nature as features of natural character, free at last from the super-imposed whims of kings, emperors and tyrants. For the Germans a war is like an overflow for a river, a periodical crisis of its ever-flowing forces. Even in normal times, the Germans "flow" in a kind of forward continuous movement (not necessarily coloured by "progress" as a sociological idea), a forward movement very much like a river in spirit, but apt in actual fact to take the shape of an army marching on. Hence the importance of the idea, of the act and of the word *marschieren* in German life. The French, on the contrary, are the most sedentary of peoples. They never feel the urge to move from their comfortable homes, where everything—meals in particular—occurs in due time and according to plan and precedents. A war is therefore for the French a most unpleasant event, not because of its dangers, for the French are brave; but because it upsets the order of reasonable life. And if they must wage a war, the French set their hearts above all on a peace that may make the next war impossible.

Hence the longing for security at the core of French foreign policy. Security is the *cri du coeur* of the sedentary man. In security, the French see the triumph of reason over the savage forces of nature unleashed by war—while the German fear in security a dam of paper and principles barring their continuous flow forward into the uncharted future.

3

GERMANY—RUSSIA

THERE is a certain likeness between the Franco-German and the German-Russian relations. To a certain extent, Russia is for Germany what Germany is for France. Just as Germany, seen from France, seems a river-like, flowing spirit, so Russia, seen from Germany, seems a flowing spirit also. The paradox may be solved by observing that while Germany is like a river which, though flowing in one direction, is held within its banks in every other, Russia is like a sea flowing in every direction of the compass.

This impression of a shoreless sea which the spirit of Russia is apt to cause may well be due to the immense plain, almost lacking in natural frontiers, which is its territory, its vastness further outstretched in winter by its white monotony. Wherever the eyes rest or the feet stop, no obstacle hinders the seeker or the traveller, who may as he wishes look or step further. Through the plain, to the horizon and beyond, the empty space solicits man to fill it. This emptiness of space dilutes its value; and as man cannot occupy space without occupying time, time itself seems to lose value as space does. Thus time, which for the German is the bed of the river of his history, and for the Frenchman one of the dimensions of his universal geometry, is for the Russian something without weight or importance, an empty form. When life flows in all the directions of space, every clear sense and even every measure of time is lost.

That is why the Russian people stands in a natural contrast with the German on the other side of the other people that is in natural contrast with the German—the French. For the Germans, time is essential, since they live in an *Ewigem Werden* or continuous becoming. For the French as for the Russians, time is not essential; but, for the French, the reason is that they see time as an intellectual category; while for the Russians, time sinks into a sea which subsumes all space and all time.

Is she European, is she not? This doubt arises only in the case of Russia;[1] and it may well be that it comes from something more substantial than a mere geographic or cartographic scruple: perhaps an instinct that refuses to recognize as European everything immoderate in quantity, everything which calls forth mass rather than quality and organization. Europe stands for quality, shadings, significant differences. This enormous, undifferentiated mass, this human sea that limits her to the East, may present certain European aspects, but seems to exclude itself from Europe precisely because of its quantity and uniformity. (No, I do not overlook its two or three dozen "nationalities." But even so.)

All this helps to explain how the psychological situation of the Russians with regard to the Germans calls to mind that of the Germans with regard to the French. The Russians are barbarous for the Germans, as the Germans are barbarous for the French. This is not based merely on historical reasons. Of course, Rome's civilization polished first the French, then the Germans

[1] And of Turkey, discussed anon.

and only last the Russians (mostly through Byzantium)—a sequence which, in itself, would do to explain the relative attitudes, just outlined, of the three peoples; but there is yet another cause, deeper and more subtle, hailing not from history but from the spirit. Civilization is the art of forms, a kind of intimate sense of forms. The French possess this sense (along with the Italians) in an incomparable degree, and for all the dimensions of life. The Germans possess it only along the dimension of time—hence their gift for History and philosophy, as well as for music, an essentially temporal art. The Russians lack this gift altogether and in all dimensions. That is why the Germans seem barbarous to the French and the Russians to the Germans.

For the same reason, the Germans came to play in Russia a part similar to that of the French in Germany—they were the teachers of forms and of civilization. The attention with which the Russians observe the Germans may also be compared with the attention the Germans feel towards the French. Finally, though with different shades, the fear, almost the anxiety, the Germans experience towards the Russians recalls the respect the French evince towards the Germans, in that, in both cases the feeling is coloured by and steeped in a certain anguishing sense of an immediate danger—the flooding of Germany by the Russian sea, of France by the German river.

Thus, along its East-West axis, from Moscow through Berlin to Paris, Europe reveals two chains of tensions: one chain of attraction, deference, imitation, directed from East to West, from Russia, through Germany, to France; another chain, of curiosity, superiority, interest, respect and fear, directed from West to East, from France, through Germany to Russia.

In this spiritual journey, Europe passes from her un-differentiated origin to her most finished differentiation; from the vast mass which is and always was sunk in a kind of natural communism, to the land of the clearly defined individual whose motto is *mon verre n'est pas grand, mais je bois dans mon verre*. Germany occupies in the spirit the same intermediate situation between Russia and France which she occupies in space. Gregarious for France, she is individualist and differentiated for Russia. Just as the French feel in the German spirit an underworld of subconsciousness which evades the light of the intellect, the Germans feel in the Russians an even deeper and primordial subconsciousness. The spiritual journey from the West to the East of Europe is therefore also a descent from the clear surface of the intellect to the depths of the human being, where forms melt into each other and individuals sink into the mass.

4

GERMANY—ENGLAND

IN order to say *I have dropped my glove*, the German says *Mein Handschuh ist hinuntergefallen*. The contrast between these two sentences symbolizes much of the tension between the English and the Germans. These two verbal forms mean the same thing. But how different their way of saying it! The Englishman has reduced the number of sounds he needs to a minimum; and he says what he means by borrowing from nature one of its vivid, lived facts, which he turns into an image, and that image into a verb, *i.e.*, an action. Drop. The sound is perfect. The image is perfect also. And there is in the natural fact at the origin of it so much life, better still, so much lived experience, that the word can be transferred to the new meaning carrying with it all the wealth of the old one. *I have dropped*. You see, hear and feel the fall.

The word *glove* is another admirable English word. It fits its meaning like . . . well, like a glove. It is close fitting. That short O, that V, the most exacting of the fricative consonants, that liquid L and that gummy G manage marvellously to convey the feeling of the tight leather glove. It is one of the many cases in which the English word is so closely adapted to what it expresses that it almost looks as if the English words for things—

mind you, only for material things—were the real names they were meant to have in nature.

Now turn to the German. *Mein Handschuh ist hinuntergefallen.* Notice the organ-like weight and sonority of the sentence, its length and that of its words. There are nineteen letters in the English one; thirty-two, nearly twice as many, in the German. The possessive *My* is now loaded with a heavy N: *Mein.* Instead of the light and elegant *Glove*, the German says *Handschuh*, i.e., *hand shoe*, a concept rather than a live word, and a heavy and ungraceful concept at that, without subtlety or humour. And finally, *ist hinuntergefallen*, which is over-explanatory, a whole treatise on the art of falling, of actual, effective falling, here at my feet, lest you have not understood it—a word for slow minds who need a lot of explaining.

Such is the first impression which the German language conveys. It is more voluminous. It needs more words, more letters. No one has expressed it better than the genius who defined the seven defects of the German language as "too many books in the language; too many chapters in the books; too many sentences in the chapters; too many words in the sentences; too many letters in the words; too many strokes in the letters; and too much ink in the strokes." The seven "defects" turn out to be seven excesses, as every man who has listened to Wagner might have guessed. Good quality, but too much of it. So with the language. The words are longer, bigger, heavier. They have more consonants than other languages for the same amount of vowels; that is more matter and less spirit, or if a less esoteric view is preferred, more material and less air.

In contrast with this heavily weighted language, English expresses a people all muscle, bone and sinew. Much of the Anglo-German tension can be explained by this fact. There is a lot of ballast in the German language which the English would never trouble to handle. Substantial, the English language is not bulky; it has body but not corpulence. It is not fat, and above all it is dry. While most of the German weight which the language reveals is not that of solid matter but rather of matter which has been swollen by being soaked in water. English is to German as a dry sponge to a soaked one. This mushy character of the German language finds expression in the superabundance of the sound *Sch*, which, as is well known, can be heard not only wherever it is written (which is often enough) but also wherever an *S* meets any other consonant; for instance in *Spät*, pronounced *Schpät*. The swelling which so much water produces adds also to the volume of the numerous syllables in um, am, em, all heavy with mush; and, at the slightest pressure, all this water fizzles out in the words ending in *Itz*, like *Spitz*, or *Witz*.

The German is moreover usually hot by temperament. Then, all this water tends to produce steam. Hence the frequency of the sound *F* in German, particularly at the end of the syllable. All *V*'s are made to blow out steam and become *F*'s. And as for *P*'s they all end in *F*'s, as in *Pferde*, *Pfeife*. No German can make a *P* explode neatly without letting off after it the surplus pressure of the steam in his soul. Thus camp becomes *Kampf*. And the very word for steam could not be more characteristic: *Dampf*.

All this would appear to show that the typically German state of mind might be that hot sentimentality which finds expression in words such as *Schwüle* and *Schwärmerei*. It is hot. One breathes with difficulty. There is a lot of foam, *Schaum*, within. It seeks an outlet, and the language becomes a *Dampfmaschine* all *Schw*'s and *FFF*'s.

A certain tension was bound to set in between the hot, *Dampf*, sentimental German and the dry, sinewy and cool Briton; a tension which need not be symmetrical. For it is plain that the dry state is more comfortable than the steamy, and so one may not unnaturally surmise that the German will envy the Englishman for his coolness and dry collar, while the Englishman would not dream of envying the German his water and steam. Nothing expresses this contrast better than their respective necks: that of the Englishman, wiry and corrugated on vertical lines, like strings and ropes commanding action; that of the German undulated on horizontal lines and in some extreme, though not rare, cases looking as if he carried under the pink skin at the back of his neck the three regulation sausages for his travels in life.

The atmosphere of hot *Dampf* turmoil vainly struggling to settle and cool down, in which the German lives, calls forth images of the early phases of the earth's life, when the surface of our planet was just beginning to fall below boiling point. And in fact the German spirit has something of this saturnine period of creation. It is ever in a state of condensation, which compensates for its state of fizz and fuzzle. Hence the ever-undefined, ever-flowing nature of the German being, vaporous, nebulous, never well defined, never well outlined, always in a state of becoming. *Werden*, to become, the word most frequently used in the German language, is as near as the German can get to express the future. The Latin languages emphatically say "I have to do something", for that is the meaning of the future which they have shaped for themselves on original lines independently of the Latin language from which they all come: *haré, ferai, farò.* The English form of the future is equally definite. *I shall do it* or *I will do it.* The German says: *Ich werde es tun,* that is: *I am becoming doing,* I am flowing from this present state of not doing into a state of doing.

This undefined character of the German soul comes out also in his curious bisexuality. His hot sentimentality does not seem to find a precise sexual outlet. He remains undecided. By no means weak, but ambivalent. Germany gives one the impression of being the country in which the sexual attraction is least defined on masculine or feminine lines. This makes of the German soul a perpetual adolescent. The way in which young men speak to young men in German works is unthinkable outside Germany for any but sexual inverts. The dialogue between Don Carlos and Posa in Schiller's absurd drama is typical. It makes Spaniards furious, contemptuous or amused about it. Now, this undefined, unpolarized nature of the German's libido fits in perfectly with the *Schwüle* of his *Schwärmerei,* with the hot-damp atmosphere of the first days of creation which is typical of his primeval soul.

The Englishman is also peculiar with regard to sex. It is a typical feature of his language that, unlike Latin and German languages, it grants no sex to things. Obviously this is the only sensible way of dealing with inanimate objects, to make them neuter, and in this at any rate, the English reveal themselves as the only logical nation in Europe . . . Hm. . . the English . . . logical! That sounds hardly credible. And of course it is not so. It is not through logic that the English have got rid of the sex variant in things, but through their empirical executive genius which has led them to simplify language by shedding all unnecessary forms. They have in fact reduced to a minimum the sex-variant or gender even in the case of human beings, so that articles, adjectives, participles and substantives are the same for male and female. And as for logic it is enough to remember that, for the Englishman, cars, cats and ships are feminine even though a warship is styled a man-o'-war and a merchant ship a merchantman.

Odd, both, in sexual affairs, the German and the English carry their oddity with a difference. For the English, sensuality is repressed, ignored and starved owing to the fact that English nature is somewhat lacking in all kinds of capacity for sensuous enjoyment, as his dancing (mostly gymnastics) and his cooking (mostly feeding) show. For the German, sensual life is distorted, mixed up and made morbid by all the dampness of his psychological morass. Hence the monstrosity of making the sun feminine, *die Sonne*, the moon masculine, *der Mond*, and the maid, neuter, *das Madchen*—three facts of the language which tell more about the German soul than volumes of philosophy.

Here again the Anglo-German tension turns out to the advantage of the Englishman; for his sensual spareness does not worry him, since he is blissfully unaware of it; while the German is steeped in his morbid sensuous sentimentality, and he envies the Englishman for his freedom from something about which he, the German, knows little that is not unpleasant.

It may well be that this formless character of the German soul is behind his tendency to devote himself to philosophy. There are of course philosophers in all times and in most lands. But the Germans stand out as the particular nation with a philosophy dealing directly with the fluid and nebulous atmosphere of thinking for the sake of thinking, and for the vigour and application they have devoted—to recall an admirable saying of Unamuno—to the art of *sculpting the mist*. There are many kinds of philosophy, and there is a world of difference between the well articulated sets of concrete arguments in a Descartes or in a Spinoza and the stream of dialectics which flows from a Kant or a Hegel. The long sentences with long-drawn rhythm and woolly profile flow in German philosophy like those rivers of music which Wagner has poured for ever over our ears and souls.

Musical philosophy and philosophic music, these two rivers flowing from the German soul are both expressions of its humid temperament, of its *Dampf*. How many *FFF*'s and *Sch*'s it is possible to throw off through the trombones of an orchestra! Wagner knew it well and Brahms even better. Music is the ideal world for the German, and Wagner's the ideal form for this world. The sarcasm with which Wagner treated Mozart—for that is, after all, the meaning of *Die Meistersinger*—is most revealing; for Mozart's soul was not German. There is no *Schwüle* in him, no *Schwärmerei*; there are in him no *Sch*'s to make simmer and bring to the boil, no *FFF*'s to let off. And so his outline is clear—outline, the most un-German of things.

Both the English and the Germans are somewhat deficient in the sense of form; but for different reasons. In the Englishman, it is due to his predominant interest in action, which leads him to distrust all kinds of fruition, and in particular aesthetic fruition, in which he sees but a diversion and a waste of energy. In the Englishman's tendency to action there is in fact something of the puritan, perhaps even of the ascetic spirit. Hippolytus before Phedra. The German, on the contrary, neglects form just as he neglects all outward life in order to take refuge in his inner being, fluid and sonorous and inwardly sensuous. The motive is therefore exactly the reverse. In one case an extreme polarization towards the outside world; in the other total introversion. That is why their deficiency in form manifests itself respectively in the Englishman as complication, accumulation, improvisation, adaptation of old forms to new ones, very much like those old ramshackle houses so typical of England, built either without a plan or with different plans at different dates on different levels, strewn all over with unexpected steps and queer corridors; in the German, merely as a mass without outline.

Hence, it is easier for the German to arrive at form than for the Englishman. Because as the Englishman goes about in the world and the sense of form does not come natural to him, when he turns his attention to it he is apt to be conscious and even self-conscious in matters of form; this leads to affectation, unless he devotes his attention to craft and materials, and then he is often excellent. For instance in printing. On the other hand in purely intellectual matters he is apt to fall into extremes, either formless or too formal and affected. Even Shakespeare, the master of all in the arts of the mind, is in this somewhat defective, and his works, nearly all admirably constructed as plays, do not shine for their inner intellectual form as works of art—not even *Hamlet*, the most poetical of all and the most musical.

The Germans, on the other hand, in music which is their art, reach aesthetic form precisely because they are "mist sculptors." Nay more. It is in the greatest of them that man has attained the highest and purest form: form without matter. Bach and Beethoven in particular, by sheer concentration of the spirit on itself, have succeeded in creating this pure and immaterial form, to a degree nowhere else attained.

All these contrasts can be explained by the attitudes which the two nations adopt towards action. The Englishman goes to action spontaneously, for his instinct tells him that he is a master in the handling of things as well as of people. The German, masterful also in the handling of things, is singularly inept in dealing with persons; and, feeling this more or less obscurely, he withdraws within himself. The powerful sonority of his inner world is but the sublimation of all the echoes of his outward failures. The wonderful flow of energy the German nation has poured over the world of music, possibly without an equal as an aesthetic creation anywhere else, measures the mighty backwash of a vigorous national soul thrown back within itself by the outer world which it has failed to conquer in repeated, disastrous sorties.

This is one of the most acute causes of Anglo-German tension; England is a successful imperial people; Germany a people that has failed to become imperial. That is why the German is ever busy studying the Englishman, hoping to discover the secret of imperial success. From the brothers Humboldt and even from the great Goethe, there is hardly an outstanding German who has not devoted much time and attention to analysing the Englishman, some of them with a sincere admiration, others with a barely disguised envy.

How pleased was Goethe when in 1827 he received a letter from Walter Scott. The opinions of Goethe on England and the English, which Eckermann notes down, throw much light on the nature of the Anglo-German tension. Although in 1825 Goethe assured an English visitor that he had been busy studying the English language and literature for fifty years, it is possible to wonder whether the "father of German literature" (as Walter Scott calls him) ever mastered the English language; for Eckermann, referring to Scott's letter, provides this curious detail: "As the English writing was somewhat illegible to him, he begged me to translate the contents to him." It seems that he might just have asked to have them read. This might explain Goethe's curious observation on the English in general: "All Englishmen are as such somewhat lacking in reflection; the dispersion of their activities and the party spirit prevent them from achieving a calm development. But they are big as practical men."

Such is the somewhat naïve opinion of a man of thought who, though bewildered at the activities of the man of action, admires him as such, and yet imagines that one can be a man of action without reflection. "To the

H

real poet"—he said to Eckermann—"the knowledge of the world is inborn, and he needs neither much experience nor much empiricism to achieve a representation of it." The contrast between the two nations could not be better put. Eckermann's context shows that Goethe was thinking of himself when he spoke of the true poet. But he knew full well how strong is the German tendency to think on thinking. For instance, to Eckermann: "Meyer often says 'if only thinking were not so difficult!'—but the worst is that thinking about thinking is never any use; one is only right if one is born to be right". And when expressing the view that poetry must always be born out of concrete reality he concludes: "I care nothing about poems conceived out of air".

He was fully aware of the direction in which a German had to strive, and why all Germany was already in a tension towards England, the people of men "great as practical". The tension is the sharper for the fact that there is a certain family relationship between the two nations, as shown in the common origin of their respective languages and even in the name *Anglo-Saxon* universally though somewhat arbitrarily given to the English. Both possess a marvellous tenacity which manifests itself in their constancy when at work and in their magnificent valour when at war. But, springing from the will as this feature does, it differs in the two nations in important aspects; for the will, its impulse and its form, are always the most direct expression of character.

The Englishman takes nothing for granted. He does not let loose his will until he has carefully taken stock of things and people. Hence his admirable balance in action. The German lives within himself and it is there, in his inner laboratory, that he draws his plans and prepares his deeds. When he sallies forth towards action, his decision is already made. Things do not resist him, for he knows them well and he is a good technician. But people do, for he is not skilful at handling them. Nothing so arouses his ire as that persons should not behave like things. Hence his failure as an imperial people. All too frequently, for the German, will-power means stubbornness and brutality. He is tenacious but, unlike the Englishman, he is not elastic.

This stubbornness of the Germans is apt to come out most curiously even in the noblest and greatest of them. Beethoven can express it; particularly in those dreadful fights in which he at times engages against the sonorous material of his symphonies with a furious exasperation which reaches its paroxysm in his endless codas, when he thrashes the poor symphony to death. Here, the German will reveals itself as a blind force of nature rather than as human energy methodically applied to an object by an intelligent and self-controlled being. It is, of course, a fact that this brutal stubbornness of the German will is a compensation for the vague and nebulous character of his inner world. Rigid without, fluid within. The mechanical discipline to which he longs to submit, the goose-step, and the military parades even for picnics, are but forms of his need of a strong social container to hold his soft being.

This parallel between Germany and England suggests a difference somewhat deeper and more essential than the trend to action on the one hand and to introspection and frustration on the other. It is as if Germany corresponded more closely to physical nature and England to social nature. Just like Germany, physical nature is intelligent in an applied, infallible and mechanical way; but wholly indifferent to moral and social values. Why? it might be objected, how about Kant and the stars and the categorical imperative? But all that forms part of the mechanical infallibility of things, of physical nature. It is the all philosophical technique of morals, not live morals. The sense of social nature, born of the soil, impure, empirical, self-ignorant, which grows little by little and takes form with time until it becomes a human society moved by moral values—that is the English way. And from here also comes in part the Anglo-German tension. "How is it possible that we who know more about morals"—ask the Germans—"should be less successful in social affairs?" They do not realise that, in social affairs, to know counts less than to will, to will counts less than to do and to do counts less than to be.

There was a time when in England it was fashionable not to see these differences between Englishmen and Germans, or at any rate to consider them as proofs of the superiority of the Germans. All likenesses between the two nations were emphasized and Latin people were looked down upon. Darwinists laid it down that the law of progress was the survival of the fittest, which in political terms became "might is right". Carlyle admired Germany, exalted the hero and chose for his model of the heroic man Cromwell first and Frederick of Prussia after. Later in the century, Rhodes founded the Trust for British, British Dominions, United States and German students—no Latins need apply. Anglo-Saxon countries enacted immigration laws carefully drafted to keep the Blond Beast unpolluted from Latin blood. In the Chairs of Philosophy and of History, little that was not German was heard with any respect. Even German militarism was envied and studied, and Lord Haldane, the great War Minister to whom Britain owes its modern armies, declared that Germany was his spiritual home.

It was then that Germany adopted England as one of the Germanic peoples. This was an old mania in Germany, already noticeable in Herder for whom the English were but Germans surrounded by sea. Of course the Germans had not noticed the *Deutschtum* of the English until England had proved herself a successful nation. Had England failed in history and in culture, England would not have been Germanic. But England was a double success: it was the Empire and it was Shakespeare. Unable to annex the Empire, the Germans annexed Shakespeare.

Anyone who has watched the movements, almost as mechanical as those of an automaton, of a soldier of the Guards, say a sentinel at St. James's Palace when he decides to walk a few steps, will hesitate before denying that the English are a Germanic people. Fortunately however for the British Isles there are three other nations in it which are not Germanic. The Scotch, the Welsh and above all the Irish have happily compensated the Germanic features of the English character. They have taught Englishmen to disobey.

This balance between the individualist spirit of its non-Germanic elements and the disciplined spirit of its Germanic elements is the true cause of the greatness and strength of Great Britain. The first World War killed the fashion of the Nordic superiority. True there still remain in Britain traces of this past; some of them legitimate, for there are indisputable features of excellence in Germany, such as for instance their technical ability which remains on the whole unimpaired even after the inept expulsion of the Jews. But there are other forms of the pro-German prejudice still lingering in Britain and which would appear less justified. A German name is still an asset not merely in science but in literature.

Nevertheless, in the main, the tension between England and Germany is above all due to an emulation and even envy of Germany towards England. The England the German admires is precisely that of the imperialist and aggressive days, that of Cecil Rhodes and Kipling; not the liberal and creative Britain, mother of crowned Republics. Even Nietzsche, in spite of his constant attacks on the mediocrity of the English, conceives his Superman mainly as a super-Englishman rather than as a super-German; but the Englishman within his super-Englishman is that contemner of "the lesser breeds without the law" who ruled the world in his days. The core of the German disease—for Germany is a diseased nation—is envy of the imperial success of England. That is why when asked for her *desiderata* in world affairs she was never able to be clear about them, and all she could do was to bleat *Lebensraum*—a typical German word with its vague spaciousness without outlines.

There is thus a certain likeness between the Anglo-German tension on the one hand and the Italo-French on the other. Germany believes that the part England plays in the world is hers by right, because the German people are more capable than the English. Such is *mutatis mutandis* within the Latin world the attitude of Italy towards France. And in both cases the tension is sharpened by the imperturbable calm of the envied one.

The second World War came to make the Anglo-German tension more complex, adding on the English side a new element: fear of Germany. The vigour, the ability, the toughness, the gregarious discipline, the mechanical and technical capacity of the Germans make up a truly formidable combination. Defeated for the second time, will they rise again? The very tenacity of their resistance gives a new zest to the Anglo-German tension at the English end.

Meanwhile Europe is nearly dying of the consequence of this tragic tension. Germany is the core of Europe. She stands at the centre of her body, at the apex of her mind, in the innermost chambers of her conscious and subconscious being, the source of her most glorious music. Philosophy, science, history, technology are unthinkable without Germany. If Germany falls, Europe falls. If Germany goes mad, Europe goes mad. The moral health of the German people is one of the chief conditions for the moral health, indeed, for the very existence of Europe.

Now, despite the Soviet danger, it is the English-German tension that remains the chief trouble in the German soul. Can it be cured?

It depends on Germany. But it depends even more so on England. If England remains in her belated state of evolution, still, despite appearances, attached to power politics, Germany will not be able to shake off her own ingrained tendencies to power politics. This will raise the electrical tension between the two peoples, bringing on both of them in the future, and on their neighbours, as many disasters as in the past. The Anglo-German'

tension must be purged of this, its most dangerous aspect;
and to this effect both England and Germany must abjure
their essential isolationism, merging themselves truly—
and not merely in gestures and words—into a Europe
they both must lead with France. But this conversion
must come about first in England.

5

FRANCE—ENGLAND

How far and how near do France and England live from each other! The closest together and the widest apart, perhaps, of any two European peoples, the French and the English are both intimate friends and keen adversaries, different and alike, ever desirous to understand each other and always at loggerheads. It is as though the basic discordance between their respective characters gave rise to such delicate and rich resonances as not to exclude a certain harmony.

This basic discordance is such as almost to preclude all permanent agreement for lack of that essential element: a mutual understanding. The incurable empiricism of the Englishman and the no less incurable rationalism of the Frenchman pre-situate them in such mutually irreconcilable perspectives as to make it almost impossible not merely to understand each other, but to prevent mutual suspicion. So far as character goes, therefore, the French and the English start from an antinomy which predisposes them to antagonism, if not to actual enmity.

On this background of so poor a promise, other less forbidding aspects fortunately come to light. France is, after all, the country that interests the Englishman most. Much explaining and shading will be needed to describe such an interest, even approximately; but, to begin with, there is no doubt that it exists and that it is widespread.

One of the roots of the prestige of France in England is the tradition nine centuries old which sees in Normandy the country of the Conquerors. To this day, the Norman King bears in history the name of William the Conqueror—a sign that history has been to this day visualized from the standpoint of the conquering Knights. Just as during three centuries the Spanish-American whites prided themselves on their descent from the *Conquistadores*, and even to this day many a Spanish American will be happy to think of his Spanish ancestry, so in England, from 1066 to this date, the tradition has remained alive that sees in the Norman the aristocrat, the rich, the master, and, therefore (with logic not always confirmed by History), the refined, the cultivated, the better man.

This tradition is reinforced by the long-drawn adventures of English Kings and Knights in France. The vineyards of Aquitania, the castles of Touraine, Chinon, Agincourt, Calais are memories that haunt the inner spaces of the English as much as they do the inner spaces of the French. The King of England called himself King of France till but yesterday.

The prestige arising from this double conquest of England first and of France afterwards, by the Norman-English aristocracy, is harvested by France. The observation has often been made that while the English names for domestic animals are Anglo-Saxon (swine, ox, calf, sheep), the meat these animals yield bears names of French origin (pork, beef, veal, mutton), because the live animals were in the care of Saxon peasants but the meat went to the table of the Norman lord. This detail reveals an initial relationship in which the French lord it over the English; and explains the incomparable prestige the French language enjoys in England, where it was for long the language of the Crown, the Court and the State. As late as the XVIIth century, English law treatises were still written in a picturesque language, legal French, a curious corruption of the language of Molière which Molière would have enjoyed. Modern English owes to this old prevalence of French a good share of its vocabulary; and French still is in England a not altogether foreign language inasmuch as a French word can nearly always be set into an English sentence without cutting a strange figure in the company.

With the passing of time, nobility turns into snobbery. Let us not, however, underestimate snobbery, for it is a powerful factor in these matters. It certainly is one of the mainsprings of the prestige of France in England; and for two reasons, one social, the other intellectual. Social snobbery hails back to those Normans. Nothing more flattering to the English wearer than a French name, particularly if slightly corrupt. A certain amount of corruption in the French of an English name is as refined a delicacy as in partridge; for a plain French name may be worn by any one who might but yesterday have been a stevedore in Rouen, while a name on its way from a French to an English form—who would display it but a scion of the Norman conquerors?

Intellectual snobbery is somewhat humbler. French is, after all, the easiest language for an Englishman to learn, since a good third of English is but French badly pronounced (table, chair, vase, bottle, city, port, route, mountain, valley, river, torrent . . .) A critic or a plain man about town with literary pretensions can always make a good show if he is able to read, and better still, to speak French. French literature enjoys in England a kind of facility-premium.

All these factors contribute to popularize the French language and nation in the aristocratic, well-to-do and cultivated circles of English life and in the wider zone of those who imitate them. These circles are of course in England the least impervious to the aesthetic aspects of life, whether the direct ones of experience or the indirect ones of art. France being the country of enjoyment, the well-to-do and cultivated English are wont to find comfort and expansion in her, the land where they forget the Puritan austerity of their country. In one word, France is for many Englishmen the teacher of sensuousness. To France they go—or dream to go —to learn to eat, love and enjoy the pleasures of art —each according to the particular direction of his own sensuality. To France they will go also to doff the social strait-jacket they wear at home and to try to be just what they are, free from the inhibitions which their strong social discipline imposes on them at home.

The adjective *French* suggests thus to the Englishman all kinds of agreeable things—if more or less prohibited or at any rate out of bounds. This ethical-aesthetical polarization between the two peoples finds an outlet in the English saying that the French have one hundred sauces but only one joke; to which the French might reply that the English have one hundred jokes but only one sauce. France reigns supreme on certain aspects of English life, such as feminine fashions. On no account would an English milliner consent to call herself Mrs.

Madame must it be, even though it may lead to such things as Madame Jenkins.

There are, however, many Englishmen—and they are by far the more numerous—for whom sensuality—be it culinary, amatory or artistic—means nothing at all. Nearly the whole people and a good part of the middle class. As for the people, their blindness towards every kind of sensuality is, so to speak, innocent. They do not even realize the existence of the world of enjoyment. They eat anything, even shepherd's pie or steak and kidney pudding or some kind of sticking-paste no bill-poster would look at, which, for some unknown reason, they describe as *porridge*, though it has nothing to do with this well-known Scotch delicacy; they drink black Indian tea, a truly infernal drink; and they reproduce themselves by a form of spontaneous generation not yet fully known to biologists. There is no lack of these "innocent" insensibles in the middle-class; but here one also comes across types more conscious of their own indifference towards the things of the mind, and even proud of it. One of them, related to an illustrious house, once said to me: "I cannot tell a Picasso from a Raphael." He was bragging.

History also influences the Frenchman's attitude towards England and the English. During the XVIIth century, the throne of the world gradually passes from Spain to France, and England's enmity follows. The XVIIIth century witnesses a protracted duel between France and England, which ends in Trafalgar. The memory of this duel is the strongest historical factor in the French attitude towards England. The days of Normandy and Aquitania have faded in the grey past; but

France does not forget that it was the English that expelled her from India and from Canada. As France,
moreover, reaches the XIXth century, and even the
XXth, weaker than England, yet still a great Power, the
struggle between them drags on till our own days, for
instance, in Egypt, until after coming to the brink of
war over Fashoda, they reach at last an agreement
under pressure from the German menace.

Whoever doubts that these two and a half centuries of
Franco-British history have left a deposit of resentment
in France, should first have a good talk with French
sailors. Towards the beginning of this century a Breton
song, popular in Paris, devoted a significant stanza to the
subject:

> Pour combattre la flotte anglaise
> Comme il faut plus d'un moussaillon,
> J'en ferons à ma Paimpolaise
> Qui m'attend au pays breton.

Under the stress of the German danger, the French
soldiers have lived down these bitter memories; not so
the sailors; and this explains that, when invaded by
Hitler, France fell into the hands of a host of admirals—
all anti-English.

France never had it in herself to understand England,
as anyone can see for himself who reads Voltaire or
Victor Hugo on Shakespeare. In her case, therefore,
many negative factors meet (historical, geographic,
psychological) working for an antagonism which does
not break into open conflict for two reasons: the first is a
common danger, German yesterday, Russian to-day; and
the second, that, by a kind of compensation, France feels
towards England a conscious and intelligent attraction

as strong as the spontaneous antagonism which lines it. The best tasters of English life, from Taine to Denis Saurat—have been Frenchmen. This explains the prestige England has enjoyed in France precisely during the two and a half centuries of struggle between them.

In part, at least, from the end of the XIXth century, this prestige of England in France has been due to sports and games. Everything in this domain was English: from its rules and its social organization to its vocabulary and its attire. The French embraced the sporting faith with the fervour of neophytes, a fervour which leads them at times to excesses in imitation, particularly in the matter of words; as when, afflicted by a kind of anglomania, they pepper their lovely language with singularly ill-chosen English words, such as "faire du footing" for rambling or walking. Sports and games determine thus a second English conquest of France which, in the pleasantest and friendliest way, brings about a far-reaching transformation of the life of the country. Once confined to his home, fond of his slippers and dressing gown, fearful of cold draughts, physically lazy, the Frenchman, under English influence, rises from his armchair, stands erect, throws away his spectacles and his carefully annotated books, and goes out into the open, younger and stronger than he knew himself to be; and soon he vies with his English model on tennis courts and golf links.

Between the two neighbouring peoples no obstacle exists to-day to prevent them from working happily together. They complete, esteem and even admire each other—but still remain at a psychological distance much greater than that which separates them on the map. And the English still refuse to build that tunnel. . . .

6

ITALY—GERMANY

THE tension between Italy and Germany is one of the
oldest in Europe, for it dates from the days of the Roman
Empire, when the wild Germans fell on the Roman
cities, looted them and left them in ashes—their population massacred or carried away to slavery. Little by
little the Germans allow themselves to be domesticated,
accepting subsidies, and even posts within the Roman
State. This was the first victory of Italian creativeness
over the formless fury of the Northerners. Charlemagne
and the three Ottos were living examples and symbols
of the same tension between the formless vigour of the
North and the tradition of beauty, order and purpose of
the South. Italy thus may be said to be the mother of
German civilization.

There are here the elements of a masculine-feminine
relationship, not unlike that which relates the masculine
genius of Spain to the feminine talent of France. The
relationship is bound at times to call forth a precipitate
flight of the weaker of the two partners—the masculine—
terrified of the powers of absorption and annihilation
which feminine charm is apt to conceal. This attitude,
which might be described as the *Potiphar* complex,
usually takes the form of a violent protest, on ethical
grounds, against the sinful snares of the Serpent every

woman is known to hide under her bed. This would
appear to be the deepest sense to be attached to Luther's
break with Rome.

In support of such a view—not the most theological,
but certainly the most biblical, so far advanced to explain the great Schism—it should be pointed out that,
on any other account, the *national* aspects of Luther
remain unexplained. How is it that this hard-headed and
rebellious friar, rebellious, that is, towards the Vatican,
but, towards his own, authoritarian and "popish,"
climbs, so to speak, overnight, to the top of *Deutschtum*
and becomes the symbol and paragon of all that is German? A mere dispute over indulgences would not appear
to warrant so much—or so little either. For Luther does
not merely break away from the Pope; he breaks away
from universality. He forms a German Church. This
shows that, in his time, Luther incarnated a profound
German instinct, antagonistic to Rome. To explain his
attitude as a protest against authority will not do, since
Luther was as authoritarian as any Pope; as a protest
against irrational creeds on behalf of reason, less still, for
Luther was irrational in the extreme, and few thinkers
ever hurled at reason insults as violent and even as coarse
as he did. Nothing remains but the peculiar panic which
seizes the masculine spirit once it allows itself to be
overpowered by the Potiphar complex.

The consequences of this shameful flight of Wotan
from the Virgin Mary, in whom his fright imagined and
guessed the dangerous snares of Venus, have proved
disastrous for Europe. Let whoever doubts it take a trip
to Germany and compare the Lutheran and the Catholic
lands; let him re-read history or recollect events, and
note that, though, officially, Hitler was a Catholic and

I

Hindenburg a Lutheran, Hitler was raised to power by the Lutherans, while the Catholics—with the prominent and notorious exception of von Papen—resisted his sway. We are not concerned here with dogma; but with the political and humanistic resonances of an attitude. By her flight from Rome, Luther's Germany severs herself from the universal spirit; her powerful spirit folds itself inwards, and acquires that redoubtable nationalism which will expose her to crises of inhuman madness.

On the German side, the tension with Italy will be found to contain the two chief elements in a masculine-feminine relationship—desire for possession, tinged with greed and brutality, and fear of being fascinated and ensnared by grace and beauty, the enemies of masculine force. Every German who goes South and discovers Italy suffers a metamorphosis. He suddenly realizes that he has been living in a boor's paradise without form, light, joy. That latinity which the old-time monks imposed on the German language like a strait-jacket from outside, making of this northern tongue a kind of imitation Latin, that latinity which had all along been in their words, but no more, they suddenly find in the churches and in the galleries and in the streets. All much the same, for the streets of Italy, are they not like galleries alive? Goethe is a symbol of this surrender of the German to the *classicism* he finds in Rome, and his trip to Rome corresponds aesthetically to the journeys of Charlemagne and the Ottos in the political field. Heine, who, as a German Jew, was well qualified to observe the Italo-German tension, wrote most acutely on this. "I do go to the Opera in order to behold the faces of the beautiful Italian women. No doubt they are beautiful enough out of the theatre and a student of the human face might well deduce from the ideal nature of their features the influence of the fine arts on the physical build of the Italian people. Nature has in this case claimed back from the artists the capital she once had lent them, and see, she has gained an enchanting interest on it. Nature who once had provided her models to the artists, in her turn now copies their master-pieces which resulted therefrom. The sense of the beautiful has imbued the whole people, and just as once the flesh worked on the spirit, so now the spirit works on the flesh.''[1]

The theme is here illustrated on the plane of physical form, on which the German, not endowed by nature with physical beauty, is of course overwhelmed on finding it so abundant in Italy; but it could equally well apply to the things of the mind; for Italy has ever been the teacher of form and style for the whole of Europe and in particular for Germany.

There is between these two nations a common feature which predestines them perhaps to a mutual attraction as well as to a certain likeness in their historical evolution. Both Germany and Italy reveal a strange resistance to coalesce into big States. This may well have been determined by the fact that Italy housed the Papacy and Germany the Empire—monarchies of an extra-national, if not universal, nature. As a consequence both Italy and Germany remained congeries of small States, until late in the nineteenth century. These small States were by no means similar. Germany's were more monarchical, Italy's more republican and unruly. But, in both cases, the feature leads to a multiplication of small capitals and courts, which fostered intellectual

[1]*Florentinische Nächte.*

life and turned people away from the international political struggle to the pursuit of ideas and forms. This parallel prepared the mutual curiosity and respect the two peoples profess to each other on the plane of culture; while at the same time pre-determining in Italy a pro-German political orientation.

For the fact is that owing to the protracted attachment of the two nations to the coral-like form of Statehood, Germany and Italy do not attain their full stature as modern nations until 1870, fully three centuries after England, France and Spain. This fact was bound to give rise to a feeling of companionship between the two, inasmuch as, owing to their late arrival, they had found already occupied all the seats at the colonial table. (Note that Japan reached a full development as a nation on the Western pattern at the same time, and the root of the totalitarian alliance of 1939 will become apparent.)

It is then that the tension between Italy and Germany takes on a new and unpleasant turn at the Italian end. The Italians had always held the Germans as barbarians until relatively modern times. Then came the impressive German conquests in the realm of the mind. The Italian, with as keen a taste for intellectual vintages as any European, soon realized the quality of this newcomer in the field, and devoted more and more attention to the literature and philosophy of Germany. At this stage, Gobineau and Chamberlain start their glorification of the Blond Beast. Leonardo was apparently to be admired not so much because he had painted St. Anne, but because, being golden-haired, he was the son, if illegitimate, of a German-blooded father. Many Italians allowed themselves to be bamboozled by this fad. Then came Nietzsche, whose peculiar ethics of the Superman was bound to appeal to many countrymen of Cesare Borgia (on his mother's side).

Meanwhile, Bismarck was raising the status of Germany to that of the most dreaded cock in the European cockpit; and Italy, deflected from her true course by the parallelism of her historical development, decided to cast her lot with the German militarists of the Second Reich. A twist, perhaps unexpected, of this parallelism between the two nations, allows Italy to continue as Germany's ally when the Second Reich becomes the Third. The masterpiece of this imitative phase was the Prussian goose-step imposed on Italian troops by Mussolini; though, of course, Mussolini had excellent grounds to consider himself as the model Hitler was imitating. But the situation that ensued can best be described in the dramatic brevity of a Spanish proverb: "To the teacher, a dagger-stroke".

Who remembers the once famous Axis, round which the two dictators made revolve a tragicomic episode of European history? Well forgotten though it is, no true European should, however, overlook the essential nature of the Italo-German axis in the structure of Europe, linking as it does two peoples who have respectively kept the Papal and the imperial tradition, and are among the most creative of our European family.

7

ENGLAND—SPAIN

THE Anglo-Spanish tension is subtle and complex. It is made up of two mutually antagonistic elements: the first, natural and positive, generating an attraction between the two peoples; the second, historical and negative, generating a mutual repulsion.

The natural and positive factor arises out of the play between the two national characters, for they are, in the main, complementary, without being altogether what one might describe as "psychological antipodes" (as is, for instance, the case with the Spanish and German characters). The Spanish character is "pathic", *i.e.*, open to the full flow of life in the personal river-bed; therefore, complementary to the English character, with its ever-present trend to action, *i.e.*, to pouring out the flow of personal energies, into the social river-bed. The Englishman's standards are ethical-social; the Spaniard's, aesthetical-personal. This contrast is apt to foster a number of mutual sympathies between the two peoples. The Spaniard admires the Englishman's discipline, freely self-imposed. It is this *free* element that appeals to the anarchistic Spaniard, who instinctively realizes that it is the self-disciplined Englishman who is the perfect anarchist. He admires also the free social order which is the outcome of such a discipline,

in one word, the Englishman's *virtue*. The Englishman admires in the Spaniard that personal dignity,
that sense of essential things, that gift for creating
beauty without actually meaning to, in which Spain
excels.

So far, the play of contrasts. But the two peoples are
also attracted to each other by certain likenesses in their
characters; in particular by a more complex and general
sense of life, a communication with nature more intimate
and profound than in the case of other European peoples;
and, consequentially, a certain mistrust of the merely
intellectual.

The geographical situation of England and Spain on
either side of France might have strengthened this
natural attraction with just as natural political links,
since nothing is more natural for any one country than
to seek support against the dangers of its own neighbour in its neighbour's neighbour. And, to be sure, that
is precisely what happened for centuries. England leant
towards Castille, while Scotland gravitated towards
France. Nature, therefore, both human and territorial,
did all in its power to make Spain and England live on the
most cordial possible terms.

But then came Christopher Columbus, and all this
crashed to the ground. The discovery of America deflected the Spanish impetus from near-by Africa to far-off
America. This determined a set of forces which for
centuries was to antagonize two peoples made to understand each other perfectly. Almost at the same time, the
divorce of Henry VIII steeled with a personal and
passional element the schismatic tendencies of the
British (at bottom, insular rather than religious); so that
the enmity towards Spain, born at first as a form of envy,

took on a religious fervour. The pirate prayed before
setting on the rich galleons of a King at peace with his
own Queen.

No self-respecting historian would deny to-day that
most of the onslaughts the Spanish fleets and harbours of
the Indies had to undergo on the part of the English were
naked aggressions made in disregard of the generally
admitted laws and customs of Christendom; nor can it
be disputed that the chief purpose of the official or un-
official wars waged by England against Spain was the
desire to take possession of that Eldorado which Spanish-
America was for centuries in the eyes of Englishmen.
Even in our own day, Winston Churchill cannot pass by
Cuba in his Memoirs without lamenting that "we"
did not take it, nor Hudson write a novel on Uruguay
without calling it *The Purple Land that England lost*. This,
by the way, is an allusion to the expeditions of Popham,
Auchmuty and Whitelocke against Buenos Aires and
Montevideo (1806-7), on which a modern military
writer comments as follows: "It is a question whether
we should not have done better to have confined our
efforts in South America to the acquisition of Montevideo
only. Buenos Aires is too far inland and a difficult place
to hold without the goodwill of the inhabitants. Montevideo might have been a second Gibraltar."[1]

It is evident, therefore, that the normal and spontaneous attitude of the average Englishman towards
Spain and her Empire was that of the "go-getter".
Time and again, the people will reveal themselves
enthusiastic supporters of the go-ahead governments,
and infuriated critics of the Governments which seek

[1] General Sir Alexander Godley, G.C.B. *British Military History
in South America*.

an understanding with Spain. The core of the anti-Spanish feeling is the City; for the core of that core was the wealth of the Indies. Reprimanded by the Government for having, of his own initiative, gone to conquer Buenos Aires, Popham was presented by the City with a sword of honour.

Still, the avowal of such a policy of aggression for possession would have been offensive to the moral sense of the country; hence the image of a cruel and oppressive Spain, an image towards which Spain herself, endowed with as many defects as most nations, contributed generously. England built up her world Empire and her supremacy at sea mostly at the expense of Spain; while their political and economic ineptness deprived the Spaniards of the bases and means to defend their own.

This historical situation determines the English attitude towards Spain; for the international conscience of the British, more developed nowadays than it used to be, feels "bruised" at the idea that for a long period stretching from the times of Queen Elizabeth to those of the second Pitt, England, in her relations with Spain, cuts in History a piratical and aggressive figure. The mere existence of Spain is thus a tacit reproach for England.

Hence the passion the English usually bring to their views on Spain and their all-too-frequent tendency to write History without due regard for Spanish sources. Here is an example among many. The author is reviewing a modern reprint of James Burney's *History of the Buccaneers of America*: "By and large, they were several generations of picturesque rascals preying from the Caribbean upon the Spaniards, who with a greater show of legality were preying upon the natives of South America; and because the English, French and Dutch Governments could for the most part only look enviously on at the loot of a New World they were never slow to turn a blind eye to buccaneering proceedings."[1] This passage is revealing in its endeavour to whitewash the buccaneers by presenting them as just a shade worse than the *conquistadores* and *pobladores* who founded and grounded the European civilization in America. That "with a greater show of legality" is a gem, for it insinuates not only that there was nothing but show in the legal order of the Spaniards but that there was some legality (if only for show) in the buccaneers.

The secret ill-humour, the irritation many Englishmen feel towards Spain, is apt to betray itself in unexpectedly aggressive, nay, insulting epithets. H. A. L. Fisher, in his *History of Europe*, a monument of incomprehension and even of ignorance of things Spanish, writing about the Catalan and Portuguese rebellion against Olivares (whom he throughout spells *Olivarez*), says: "Iberian mountains and Iberian men are obstinate things. Olivarez ignored the mountains and attempted to drive the men. Against such an affront to its cherished quiet and seclusion no race in the world can be trusted to react with a higher degree of mulish obstinacy than the Iberian."[2] Why mulish? Is resistance to a tyrant mulish?

The mule comes also to the imagination of another English historian, having to express an opinion about Henry VIII and Catherine of Aragon. A. L. Rowse is

[1] *The Times Literary Supplement*, 21.vii.50.
[2] Vol. I, p. 628.

commenting on this Spanish woman who, after twenty
years of a happy marriage, in a Catholic world, as yet
un-split in its orthodoxy, refused to step down and allow
her husband to marry his mistress; and this is Rowse's
psychological contribution to the subject: "She took
after Isabella the Catholic, devout, austere, orthodox
[this, in 1520, is a gem], obstinate as a Spanish mule."[1]
(It is, of course, well known, that Spanish mules are
particularly stubborn.)   What a neat revelation of the
irrational root of that irritation before the Spanish
obstinacy in remaining there on record, a witness of the
coarseness and of the physical and moral cruelty of the
English King. The book he is reviewing, by an American,
emphasizes the gay, loving and dignified character of
Catherine. But no; mule she must be for refusing an
indignity which even in our days of matrimonies un-
hallowed by an ancient faith, no self-respecting woman
would have undergone.   And when another author,
bearing an illustrious name,[2] will write a Life of Mary
Tudor, she will call it "*Spanish Tudor—Bloody Mary*", a
clear suggestion that the "bloody" character of Mary
came from her quiet and charitable mother and not from
the beefy, barbarous Henry, stained with the blood of
two of his wives, and of every man who stood in his way,
beginning with Sir Thomas More.

These passages, let me say again, picked among many,
must be dwelt upon, for it is imperative to purify Anglo-
Spanish tensions by exposure. Lest any English reader
imagine that they are unduly stressed, may I quote an
almost incredible passage from H. A. L. Fisher? "Later,
when Madrid (which was only a hunting lodge in the

[1] *The Observer*, 15. iii. 1942.
[2] Mary Prescott.

Middle Ages) became the capital of a great empire, the patronage of foreign artists was extended upon a lavish scale by the sovereigns of the Habsburg house. Great models were then proposed for the imitation of the Spaniards. Titian could be seen at Madrid. El Greco worked at Toledo. But whether it was from some native vulgarity, which undervalued paint and canvas for their cheapness, or because of a certain strict and sombre religiosity in the Spanish temper, defining certain subjects only as worthy of the brush, there was no popular flowering of the painter's art in Spain. Perhaps there can be no such flowering save when thought and fancy can play in freedom. Velazquez was an exception, preaching no doctrine, constrained by no convention, and daring, a solitary among Spaniards of his age, to paint only what he saw."[1] And to think that he had that unforgettable Zurbarán in the National Gallery!

Nor should the other side be forgotten. All things Spanish exert on the imagination of the English a peculiar fascination. The word itself—Spanish—though to be sure rich in negative resonances (such as *cruelty*) is no less rich in positive associations—such as nobility, dignity. With what splendid glow does it illuminate the scene in the famous lines of an Anonymous XVIth-century poem:

> Yet if His Majesty, our sovereign lord,
> Should of his own accord
> Friendly himself invite,
> And say 'I'll be your guest to-morrow night,'
> How should we stir ourselves, call and command
> All hands to work! 'Let no man idle stand!'

[1] *A History of Europe*, vol. I, p. 373.

'Set me fine Spanish tables in the hall;
See they be fitted all;
Let there be room to eat
And order taken that there want no meat.
See every sconce and candlestick made bright,
That without tapers they may give a light.'

England occupies the first place at any rate in time,
perhaps also in eminence, among the nations whose
attention was turned to the genius of Spain. Lord
Carteret it was who commissioned Don Gregorio Mayáns
to write the first Life of Cervantes—before any one,
even in Spain, had thought of it. English was the first
translation of Don Quixote. Towards the end of the
XVIIIth century, a galaxy of English poets turned their
enlightened attention to the great works of Spain, and
Southey, Wordsworth and Shelley wrote on Spain with
affection and admiration. This Spain is never absent
from English literature, though, characteristically
enough, it remains nearly always confined to poetry,
dance and the novel, leaving History unaffected and dour.

In their turn, Spaniards do not look upon England and
the English in a uniform and general way. In this, as in
so many other things, Spain reveals her double personality, what Unamuno used to call her "Manichean
fate". The (political) Right is anti-English, partly
because it dwells more on past history than the Left.
This Left, owing to its political and religious liberalism,
is pro-English, unless it has become afflicted with
Marxist measles. Despite the persistent enmity of
England, this pro-English trend appears in Spain relatively early and in a somewhat unexpected quarter: the

Benedictine Feijóo (1675-1754) was an assiduous reader and admirer of Bacon, and in his critical writings he bestowed high praise on the English, whom, at times, he seems indeed to place above all other European nations for their intellectual achievements. From then on, despite the vicissitudes of History, the prestige of England and the English will increase until our day, among the most enlightened part of the liberal professions; while, for shallower reasons, the well-to-do, whether noble or snobbish, also tune their forks on Big Ben.

As for the people, its attitude towards the English, uncomplicated by History, culture or snobbery, is human, realistic and immediate. Proverbially, creditors in Spanish are known as "Englishmen", so that a man with many debts is said "to have many Englishmen". This would appear to be an effect of misplaced liberalities in Spain on the part of Englishmen as yet uncontrolled by their now omnipresent Exchequer. The Spanish people look upon the English with a sympathy not exempt from certain quiet mirth at his cranky or freakish ways; for it seems plain to the average Spaniard that one cannot be English without being somewhat queer and even downright mad. This is a matter of plain observation for the Spanish people. Here is a story that will give point to it.

In the outskirts of a big village, almost a small city, of Andalusia, an Englishman walked about one day, tall, ungainly, dressed in a golf suit, one of those Englishmen, standing offences against all the laws of beauty and elegance, whom England, the land of elegant men, seems to reserve for export. The unsoaped of the village, in their unconscious yet definite capacity of guardians of public beauty, began to chastise him with jokes, catcalls and even, in the Spanish saying, gutter-soup, *i.e.* . . . stones. An old peasant turned up, one of those neat Andalusian men, Seneca-faced, Tacitus-tongued. He frowned at the youngsters, and quietly admonished: "Come, children. Leave him alone. It is not his fault, poor man, that he is English!"

At bottom, therefore, the attitude of the Spanish people towards the English does not exclude a certain pity. Whence? Almost certainly from a certain awareness of the Englishman's thraldom to practical and useful things, with the sacrifices and humiliations which it entails. To which, the Spaniard, in the glory of his inner liberty, comments: "And all that trouble just to make a dead man!"

This is perhaps the deepest aspect of the Anglo-Spanish tension. The people of action and of useful things facing the people of passive and of ever-useless things—a tension which in itself could have been most fertile for both and for Europe, and may still be so, if it sheds its religious and political impurities.

8

ENGLAND—ITALY

THIS is one of the simplest tensions in Europe. Its chief element is a mutual admiration going from England to Italy in the aesthetic and cultural field, and returning from Italy to England in the political and social. The first is by far the oldest of the two, for England was aware of Italy far earlier than Italy was of England. This is only natural, for Italy had been the political capital of Europe since the days of the Roman Empire and its spiritual capital for centuries, while England was still one of the most remote countries of Christendom. When Shakespeare is familiarizing the people of London with Italian places and persons, Giordano Bruno visits England with the air of a man who, from the centre of civilization, ventures out into the wilderness. His description of life in Oxford, for instance, is far from flattering. As for the English language, he declares he is not interested, since everybody of quality in England speaks Latin, French, Spanish or Italian.

England has never wavered in her admiration for Italy as the mother of the arts. Her aristocrats, her poets and her artists have always considered the visit to Italy as an indispensable phase in their education. Dante, Petrarca, Boccaccio are probably more read and better studied in England than in any other European nation, and the

Italian classic masters of the plastic arts are, in an odd but definite way, more, so to speak, officially recognized as models in England than anywhere else.

In this fascination the English feel for Italy, elements will be found that bring to mind the similar admiration felt in England towards France. For Italy also can teach the English that sense of form in which they are somewhat lacking, that precision in outline, and that terseness in colour which does not seem to come natural to them. There is, perhaps, even more to it than that. For what the English often seek in Italy is the aesthetic approach to life, inborn in the Italians, but, in the English, often an acquired feeling, an imitative attitude.

What in the Italians is a free, spontaneous power, springing from within, capable at every moment of creating its own norms and forms, is often for the English a longing which seeks satisfaction in forms clearly set, and in norms already established. Thus it is that one finds sometimes in England more knowledge of, more respect and appreciation for the Italian classics, be it Dante or Tintoretto, than in Italy itself.

While Italy breeds artists, England breeds aesthetes. These Englishmen, fond of lovely things, often supremely intelligent and well informed, at times, also, futile and tiresome like fireflies, sooner or later find their way to the sunny cities of their spiritual fatherland. They can point to illustrious predecessors—to Byron and to Shelley, who left the shores of Britain shaking their shoes to leave behind the last grain of its utilitarian sand, and fled to the beauty and sunny skies of the Mediterranean. This type of Englishman Italianate, one of the permanent fixtures of our Europe, was once decreed by *vox populi* to be "the devil incarnate". Perhaps not

K

altogether unfair, for the Englishman's virtue is far more a social than an individual faculty, and is apt to wither away in communities other than his own, particularly when such communities are built on aesthetical rather than on ethical standards—as is the case with Italy.

Hence, perhaps, the affectation that afflicts some of the English forms of life more or less imported ready-made from Italy. The pre-Raphaelite movement is a case in point. This kind of effect is to be expected whenever England is exposed to the influence of a Latin nation: it can be observed in Anglo-French and in Anglo-Spanish relations; but it is at its strongest in the case of Italy, because it is in Italy that art is to be found in its most concrete form, with a clarity of outline and a fullness of colour that appeal to the concrete, earthbound character of the Briton.

It may also be that in the attachment of the English to Italian life there lingers also that very English feeling that a gentleman must be familiar with the Latin classics. Why, it is here it all happened—says the (never fully) grown-up Eton boy wandering about where Cicero orated, Caesar commanded and Catilina conspired; whereupon, a tender sentiment warms his heart towards that Italy, the haunting ground of the classic spectres of his youth.

In the political field, the air is clear between Italy and England. For England, Italy was never a rival; for Italy, England was never the foreign master, as Spain was, or the foreign invader and depredator, as France was. True, Mazzini might have found more sympathy in the London Home Office, but, even if they opened his letters, he can hardly have preferred England to any other political refuge had he not felt safer there than elsewhere; and, whatever the official attitude of the British State, that of the British nation was warm and friendly towards the Risorgimento. In Italy, as in most other European lands, England had a well-earned prestige as the forerunner of political freedom and democracy; the country that first made the mistakes and first (and sometimes only) corrected them. That England was the political tutor of liberal Italy from the Risorgimento until the evil days of Mussolini can hardly be disputed.

To this collective prestige should be added the deference individual Englishmen gained in Italy during the heyday of British prosperity, when the well-to-do, well-educated, and ever curious Englishman fed more than half of the tourism of Europe. It is safe to say that for one Italian who visited Britain, ten Britons visited Italy; so that, for most Italians, the Englishman they knew was that of the upper-middle classes. This, in its turn, was bound to contribute to the high opinion the Italians entertained of Britain—for, the Italians tend to judge people on aesthetic grounds and, by such a standard, only the higher levels of English society can pass muster.

The tension between Italy and England need not have known dark days. Trouble, however, began when Mussolini launched his country towards an imperial adventure which was bound to come to grief, if only because the poor Duce, who thought himself an innovator, was late by about a century, and tried to launch a new Empire in the era of the downfall of the old ones. The error was explicable, and the more easily explained by observing that it was committed simultaneously by Italy, Germany and Japan. What other feature unites these three countries? That the three of them came of age as modern States towards 1870. Their imperialism, therefore, was but the petulant assertion of a newly acquired national consciousness, seeking satisfaction immediately after its emergence in history—exactly as the imperialism of Spain, France and England three centuries earlier. Mussolini's mistake consisted in not realizing that he lived in a non-imperial age. He had no political genius. He was just copying British politics, importing a ready-made British imperialism; just as Watts and Burne-Jones were importing ready-made Italian art into England. He, the arch-enemy of England, was modelling himself on Cromwell and the Pitts as English Victorian painters modelled themselves on Raphael.

The episode—but for the terrible consequences it entailed when Hitler made the same mistake—was futile. For the first time in history, Italy and Britain shot at each other. Words were said on both sides that should have remained unsaid; and two nations which had lived in friendliness for centuries were estranged and embittered. Beneath it all, however, the friendliness remains; even though a certain sense of injustice rankles in the hearts of many Italians. But in so far as these feelings are a hangover from the days of unrestricted national sovereignty, whose end is in view, it may be assumed that the strong links of sympathy that unite Italy and Britain may be among the most constructive factors in the future of Europe.

9

GERMANY—SPAIN

In point of character, the Germans and the Spaniards
stand poles apart. The cause may be deep enough to be
put in the old formula of the four elements. If we seek
to apportion these four elements to an equal number of
European peoples, we should probably say that the
English are akin to earth, the French to air, the Germans
to water and the Spaniards to fire. No two more opposite
elements could be found than fire and water. The first
impression the Spaniard gets on reading Goethe and
Schiller is that the Germans are singularly prone to melt
into tears. One does not weep in Spain. But there is
more to it than that. The natural motion of water is
along the line of the earth, as low as possible; while the
natural motion of fire is upwards and against all there is
there to block the way of the ascending flames. Thus we
are guided from the outset to that characteristic opposition between the German and the Spanish character:
continuity and obedience in the German; discontinuity
and disobedience in the Spaniard.

Both Germans and Spaniards are more attached to the
beginning of things. We have seen that feature clearly
emerging in the Germans when contrasted with the
French, a nation close to the end of things, to their
finish and polish. But while in the Germans this link

with the beginning refers to time, it refers to space in the case of the Spaniards. The Germans feel in touch with their source through the continuous flow of the river of their collective life; the Spaniards, every one of them, separately, feels the beginning of things in the native and pristine impetus of fire that rises in him.

This contrast between an original sense flowing from the past and an original impulse rising from below is manifest in the two languages. German is, of all the chief languages of Europe, the one in which the letter *U* is most frequent. Thus, the English prefix *in* is *un* in German; and the English suffix *ing* is *ung* in German. *U* is the original vowel *par excellence*. The original sense of things has in no language a more adequate expression than the German prefix *Ur*. The physical suggestion conveyed by the prefix *Um* is typical of the fluid nature of German thought. The length and weight of the words adds to the impression; and the manner of handling separate particles of verbs, leaving them for the end of the phrase, sometimes a very long one, shows again that German thought can remain fluid and in suspense for a longer time than that of any other European.

This weight of the German language comes from the predominance of consonants over vowels, perhaps the highest in European languages, certainly so if only the chief of these languages are considered. Here, again, German and Spanish stand poles apart, for Spanish is perhaps the richest in vowels of all the languages of Europe, thus suggesting the gaseous character of fire. By "richest in vowels" is here meant the feature exactly opposite of that just observed in German, the predominance of vowels over consonants in any given page. There is another sense in which the phrase could hardly apply to Spanish. English, for instance, has a high number of different vowel sounds, and is perhaps, in this sense, the richest in vowels of all the languages of Europe; but Spanish is most indigent in vowel sounds. It really has no more than five straightforward, A, E, I, O, U, in their simplest phonetic value. This again suggests that spontaneity and simplicity of a fire just springing from the soil, with no continuity, no tradition to breed subtlety. This spontaneity turns up in the very name of the nation—Spain—for the combination *sp* is characteristic of all that *sp*rings in sudden *sp*urts from the soil.

There is, for all that, a Germanic element in Spain, since several waves of Germanic tribes invaded her territory after the downfall of the Roman Empire. In the Cantabric fastnesses of Asturias, and in the *rías* or fjords of Galicia, one comes across pure Germanic types and oddly teutonic Christian names. Of all these tribes, the Visigoths were the most numerous and successful; and the monarchy which they founded has left profound traces in the history and in the law of Spain. The great Castillian heroes, notably the Cid, were Gothic in body and soul. As late as 1520-40, the Conquistadores are for the most part, as was the Cid, fair-headed and blue-eyed. These Conquistadores were bearded, and so was the Cid; but, while in the case of the medieval hero, the beard was a Germanic fashion come into Spain with the Visigoths, in that of Cortés, Pizarro and the rest, it was due to a second wave of Germanic influence, brought in by Charles V; for, between the two, the Spaniards had returned to their genuine national habit of shaving off beard and moustache.

This trifling detail is significant of the tension between the old Spanish stock and the Germanic immigrant.

This tension was for long in Spain—even though sub-consciously—associated with that between the nobility and the other classes. By tradition, the nobleman was a Goth. Hence the fact that in the novel, drama and poetry of Spain, no dark-haired, black-eyed heroine will be found until the nineteenth century; all are fair-haired and blue or green-eyed. This is a clear suggestion of the prestige of Germanic blood in Spain.

The Germanic nobility, however, were Spanish for all their Teutonic ancestry, as shown by the austerity they were able to teach the Germans of Germany when Charles V gave them an opportunity to intervene in European affairs. For those Spaniards who, as generals, viceroys, ambassadors and imperial secretaries, governed Europe for about a century did more than provide the fashion which was to rule men's and women's attire from about 1540 to about 1650; they cleaned the stables and the pigsties which many a court and noble house of Europe, and especially of Germany, had become. The strait-laced, rigid discipline of their behaviour, etiquette and even dress, was but the outward form of an inner austerity which imposed respect.

Possibly owing to the close relationship between the time of Spanish hegemony over Europe and that of Spanish intolerant orthodoxy, the Catholic, conservative Right became attached to this German connection. This purely fortuitous association was strengthened in modern days when the French revolution made France pass from the ranks of the conservative to those of the revolutionary nations. In this way, a pro-German opinion—it is not set and organized enough to be described as a party—grew mostly on religious grounds against "freethinkers and freemasons" and all that the

French Republic stood for, and won over the military also, when Germany, under Prussia, became ''an army that owns a nation.'' The reactionary side of Spain, with its two strains, the militarist and the clerical—found in Germany its spiritual home. There was, of course, in this admiration for Germany a good deal of desire for the opposite form of life. Anarchist, disobedient Spain longs for the gregarious ways of obedient Germany. One of the forms this feeling takes is the admiration felt in Spain for German technique. The Spaniard is by nature too rebellious, too impatient, to submit to the long discipline, to the *obedience to things* which the learning of a technique implies.

Thus can be explained another period of German influence on Spain wholly independent of the link between the military-clerical Spain and the reactionary Prussia. From about 1860, a leading Spanish intellectual, Professor Sanz del Río, begins to import into Spain a special kind of German philosophy—that of Krause. Why Krause? In a land as rich in philosophers as Germany, Krause did not rise above the third rate. But it happened that Sanz del Rio found in his philosophy an echo of his own Spanish intellectual trends; and in particular that sense of concrete and complete man, the most Spanish thing that can be. And so Krause became the prophet of the cultural Spanish rebirth. His influence reached through Don Francisco Giner to the present age led by the great Castillejo.

It may be noticed that this excellent German influence on Spain gave forth the third crop of beards in our country. The first was that of the Goths—with the Cid as its prototype; then came that of the imperial men— with Hernán Cortés for its prototype; the last, that of the "Institucionistas"[1]—with D. Fernando de los Rios for its prototype. But this exuberance of hair lasted little more than half a century. When Don José Ortega y Gasset returns from Marburg, where he has sat at the feet of Hermann Cohen, he brings many ideas but no hair on his chin. Unconquerable Spain emancipates herself for the third time. In Berlin, groups of young Spanish intellectuals, led by Ramiro de Maeztu, pore over Kant with so much enthusiasm that even their usual Spanish café meeting or *tertulia* becomes "la Kantina"; but they seek to compensate for the Germanization of their brains by tormenting the honest tramway conductors of Berlin with a studied conspiracy to drop out of the tram before it stops and commit every other possible breach of the Germanic *Verboten*.

Yet the fact is that all this rebellious Iberian attitude towards everything that means discipline, in so far as it manifests itself in contempt for technical mastery, may well have been the true cause of the fall of Spain as a great power. The view might be ventured that this fall of Spain can be traced to the gradual absorption of her Germanic element into the general Iberian stock; and that the true approach to a rebirth of Spain might well be the restocking of the country with German blood.

It so happens that a liberal injection of Iberian blood into Germany would almost certainly improve, indeed, save the German people as well. For the history of the last one hundred years has shown that the Germans are too gregarious and too nationalistic for the health of Europe: so that they would benefit from a blood alliance with the most individualistic and universal of all European peoples.

[1] From the Institución Libre de Enseñanza, a free college created by D. Francisco Giner.

PART IV

EUROPEAN RESONANCES

1

THE IRISH

TOWARDS 1931 or '32, when one could still, now and
then, lift one's head and smile, I arrived in Geneva for a
meeting of the Council of the League of Nations. Sir
John Simon (as he was then) was Foreign Secretary and
Mr. Anthony Eden his assistant. They asked me to lunch
at their hotel. When the meal and the Council agenda
had both been consumed, I pulled a long face and began
to address Sir John in earnest and grave tones. "You
have harassed our American Empire communications
with your pirates and sailors for three centuries; you
have backed our Spanish-American separatists and finally
destroyed our Empire; you struck us off the list of
great powers at Verona; you stole Gibraltar from us in
circumstances . . . but let that be; you backed the
United States against us in 1898 and closed the Suez
Canal to our ships; you let us down in Morocco and in
Tangier——" Sir John and Mr. Eden were nonplussed.
I waited a few seconds: " . . . very well. We are
quits. We gave you de Valera."

I was far too modest. For I should have said: "We
have given you the Irish"; since it is my considered
opinion that the Irish are Spaniards who have lost their
way and got stranded in the North, where they do not
belong. That is why they are the only Northern Catholics

and the most unhappy of all the Northerners. All Northerners are unhappy—that goes without saying; but the other ones are unhappy, so to speak, in their own right and as a matter of nature; while the Irish are unhappy as a matter of accident and as the outcome of a tragedy—that fatal mistake that took them northwards from their native Spain.

Whether the history of remote days throws any light on this event or not is a matter on which I know nothing. The grounds for my belief in the ''Spanishness'' of the Irish are deeper than any opinion based on fossil facts can ever be: they result from the direct intuition of what the Irish are and ''taste'' like to the living man who observes them. Nor are these grounds for my belief so arbitrary as to lie beyond the realm of verification, as another memory of Geneva may show.

There was an international luncheon going on, precisely in the same hotel in which my previous story had taken place; and, between the trout and the veal cutlet, I found myself explaining to my neighbour one of my favourite points: that the difference we Spaniards make between *to be in essence* (ser) and *to be in state* (estar) reveals a profound feeling of being, with a corresponding lack of any sense of *becoming* for which idea there is no Spanish word. I was just beginning to develop these views, and had so far merely stated that Spanish, Catalan and Portuguese were the only languages I knew that discriminate between *ser* and *estar*. Mr. de Valera, who sat opposite, broke in: ''We also have those two verbs in Erse.'' So I at once: ''And how do you say *to become*?''—''*To become*? . . . *To become*? . . . We have no word for *to become* in Erse.''

So, let us give a well-deserved rest to all those stories

about Spanish sailors from the Armada, who are supposed to have populated every cove in Ireland where girls are temperamental and bright-eyed—*i.e.*, every cove in Ireland. Most of the Spaniards who landed were speedily dispatched to the other world by the English land forces, anyhow. But the chief point is that the Irish needed no Spanish sailors to be as Spanish as they can be.

For, of course, one cannot be quite as Spanish as one should if one persists in living so far North century after century. Clouds will tell, and a certain amount of that constant rain must eventually get into the blood. Poteen is but a poor apology for wine, and black tea is just black despair in a cup. Thus, the Irish are less immune to inebriation than the Spaniards; and this betrays in them both a closer bondage to their conscience and to their awareness, and a lesser capacity for getting rid of the watch of these two exacting sentinels.

For your drunkard and even your drinker is not merely a vicious man who swills himself because he cannot help it, or out of spite for his maiden aunt. A drunkard is a man who wants to get rid of himself and is unable to do so by other means, such as sleep, religion, dancing, singing or communism. The Spaniard can always seize hold of a guitar. But then, the guitar is a feminine instrument that will not give itself easily; it wants one of those warm nights such as one can enjoy in Spain nearly the whole year round. Nature, in Ireland, is not so kind. And then, with all that stay-indoors weather, the Irishman grows a conscience and thinks about all kinds of things people need not trouble about in a good climate.

Worst of all, Irishmen are deeply anglified. They do not enjoy being told so, of course, but that only confirms how anglified they are, for otherwise they would not care a rap either way. They take pride in their Georgian houses, and have developed a highly "British" nationalism; by which I do not merely mean that they want to be a nation, *i.e.*, that they feel different and want to be different; but also that they want to clothe their nation with a State that must fit it tightly, as do the English. Also in imitation of the English, they have learnt a tremendous amount of political economy, which, of course, has increased their spleen and melancholy. This anglification of Ireland is not merely the outcome of centuries of English domination; but also of the inflow of English blood—hence that thoroughly un-Spanish, yet thoroughly Irish type, the jolly, beefy, beery, round-faced, rosy-cheeked, heavy-weight Irishman, one of the most picturesque cross-breeds Europe has produced.

There is another cross-breed in the Island, tougher by far than the good-humoured and well-fed Anglo-Irishman. The Belfastman, or as he, somewhat ambitiously, prefers to call himself, the Ulsterman, is an Iro-Scot, whose Scottish stock is of the dourest that even Scotland can produce. Domineering, efficient, positive and indifferent towards ideas or ideals, the Belfastman has created in Ireland a prosperous and businesslike enclave from which he looks down on the rest of the Island with a mistrust not unmixed with fear. Leaning on Great Britain in his defence against absorption, the Belfastman is at the core of the Irish problem and his toughness explains why this problem should have remained unsolved despite the agreement signed between Dublin and London to conjure it.

One more story (they seem to crop up as soon as one touches the Irish). I was at lunch (and this, please note, is the third lunch and the third story) next to an Irish author. It was a P.E.N. Club gathering. The chief point at such meetings of authors is to prevent the awful revelation that neither man has read the books of the other. So, I steered the conversation to Ireland, and, not without some pride, told my neighbour how, within two hours of Lloyd George's decision to discard the "Black and Tan" policy and come to terms with the Irish "rebels", I had gathered at my table in the Spanish Club, Cavendish Square, Art O'Brien (Irish republican agent in London) and Tom Jones (Lloyd George's Grey Eminence); "and that"—I concluded proudly—"was the beginning of the Irish Treaty." To which the Irishman answered: "You ought to be ashamed of yourself."

Had I been an Italian or a Frenchman, I should have embraced him for joy. But, no. Of course I should not, since my reason for such an extraordinary behaviour—namely, to find how Spanish the Irishman was—would have vanished had I been a Frenchman or an Italian. I did feel the joy, but being an undemonstrative Spaniard, I sat quietly for a few seconds, then I roared with laughter. "That is it," I said, "fellow-Spaniard, you wanted a civil war."

This explains how one of the heroes of the Spanish Civil War of 1876 was an Earl of Tyrone, who, as the victor of one of the Carlist battles, was granted by the Queen of Spain the title of Marquess of the North. This time, the "North" was not that into which his countrymen had strayed in bygone days, but the North of that Spain where the noble Earl had fought and where he had remained by a kind of homecoming. Spain is full of Irish names, and one of her Generals and Prime Ministers of the XIXth century was an O'Donnell.

L

Once in Spain, the Irish shed their anglification, forget about whiskey and tea, drink Christian wine and that clear fresh water which is perhaps even more than wine itself the natural drink of Spain, and become happy again—again, I mean, after the centuries of exile in the North which their misguided ancestors had inflicted on them.

But there remain their countrymen, there, in the North, nursing a grievance which may take this or that (usually anti-English) form, but is at bottom due to their resentment at being so far North when they really are Southerners. One bold solution might be to send them all to Germany; for the Irish would teach the Germans to disobey, and if the Germans learnt how to disobey, Europe might perhaps be saved. The idea is tempting. But it might have disastrous results. For if the Irish were ever to disappear from the history and destiny of England, the English themselves might forget the little disobedience the Irish have taught them. And that might be the end of all things.

2

THE IRISH—THE POLES—THE SPANIARDS

THAT sense of relief, that freshness which make a delight of any meeting with any true Irishman come from his familiarity with the absurd. By dint of passing and re-passing through the mind, the sensible becomes in the long run as irrespirable as confined air many times breathed and rebreathed. When we come to the absurd, we open our chests and breathe in. This fami-liarity with the absurd is a somewhat rare quality in Europe, perhaps only known to the Irish, the Spaniards and the Poles. Nor are their "absurds" of the same quality and flavour, even though they spring from the same root. The root is, of course, a superabundance of the individual, as against the social, pole of the being. On this, Irish, Spaniards and Poles are in perfect unison. A case in point is that of the famous Master Ferreras (he was famous in Madrid, and I am not quite sure what he was Master of) who, one day, walking in a public park heavily coated and his mouth protected by a handker-chief, read on a public thermometer that the tempera-ture was very warm—to which he heroically retorted (at the thermometer) through the handkerchief: "It is cold, whatever thermometers may say."

This determination to suffer no law, no pressure from

the world outside one's own skin, is common to the Irish, the Spaniards and the Poles. Which, by the way, explains why they are the three European peoples to possess one peculiar military quality—that of fighting on when they know that the game is up. Other Europeans, traditionally tough soldiers, the English and the Germans in particular, know how to fight to the bitter end and to refuse to acknowledge defeat; but, if they do think they are defeated, they stop fighting. Only the Spaniards, the Irish and the Poles fight on when they know it is to no purpose. It is the absurd in them that exults in a kind of glory over death.

In many other ways their absurds differ. The Irish express theirs in the form of Irish bulls, strange animals which, as is well known, differ from ordinary bulls in that they are always pregnant. The Irish bull charges at every idea he sees with the deliberate intention of goring it before having as much as smelt it. In the absurd of the Irish there is a predisposition to attack which in itself presupposes a person to be attacked. The core of the Irish absurd is a certain pugnacity, the seed of which, again, may be that resentment of the Southerner trapped and tricked by his fate in the North.

The Spaniard's absurd arises out of a refusal to admit that the world outside has a right to differ from what the man inside has decided it *is*. There is no question of "should" or "ought" here. The Spaniard is no moralist. He decides, not what the world should be, but what it is. And he refuses to admit that the world is otherwise than the shape his decision has determined. His absurd comes from this negative, which Cervantes has incarnated in Don Quixote. There is no aggressiveness here; rather a certain pity towards an outside world foolish enough to insist on going its own way instead of the way the Spaniard is sure it is going. This sentence is absurd, you say. Of course. That is what I am talking about.

In the Pole's absurd there is more flourish and panache. Sometimes far more panache even than clothes or food. The Poles love the superfluous more than the necessary, refinement more than comfort. An American beauty who, in her metamorphoses, had been a Polish princess before becoming a Hungarian countess, told me once in Vienna, that as she arrived to spend a week-end in a princely country house in Poland, the steward solemnly delivered into her hands a stick, a lantern and a mask. She asked for explanations. "Madame, the conveniences are at the far end of the garden. Should you need to travel so far in the night——" The steward broke off, thinking all would by now be clear. "The lantern I understand, but the stick?"—"You might meet a dog," explained the steward. "But the mask?" —"You might cross another guest," answered the steward.

Am I wrong in believing this story to be typical of the peculiar form the absurd takes in Poland? It is imbued with that aloofness, that distinction, that superciliousness and even that touch of impertinent disdain which one can read in Polish smiles—the most complex of all the smiles to be culled in the European garden. It tells of the contempt for what is necessary, immediate, efficient, relative; and of the quest for the superfluous, the remote, the satisfying, the absolute; it illustrates the heroic incapacity of the people to live for a country for which they can so superbly die.

3

THE RUSSIANS—THE SPANIARDS—
THE ENGLISH

THE three most intelligent nations of Europe are the French, the Germans and the Italians. I mean specifically intelligent. These three nations are the most capable wielders of reason in Europe, and therefore, in the world. This is, however, a dangerous privilege. For reason is a vehicle to convey spiritual goods from one part of the mind to another; and if you become specialized as a conveyer you may not count for much as a producer. In other words, the French, the Italians and the Germans, by their very excellence in intellectual life, might have been doomed to sterility in the realms of the spirit. From this fate they have been saved by the influence of the three maddest nations of Europe: England, Spain and Russia.

England, half-Oceanic; Spain, half-African; and Russia, half-Asiatic; these three European though not wholly (or not merely) European nations, open in the European intellect three vistas beyond the merely rational, a circumstance which gives rise to a "resonance" between them similar to that which a common familiarity with the absurd sets up between the Irish, the Spaniards and the Poles. Though the Spaniards figure in both groups, and though there is a subtle connection between a tendency to the absurd, and madness, a distinction should be made between the two sets. The "absurd" group are in revolt against the reasonable; the mad group, against the rational.

Here again every nation wears its madness with a difference though it springs from a common root. This common root is a faculty the three peoples possess, of sensing the irrational and deriving sustenance from it. But, beyond this common feature, the English, the Russians and the Spaniards are mad in three different ways.

The English enjoy madness as a liberation from their usual objectivity. Endowed by nature with a remarkable gift for assimilating the irrational, they transmute both thought and emotion into a kind of amalgam admirably plastic for purposes of action, and so become the most reasonable of nations. (It is this, by the way, which arouses the anger of the Irishman, who hates reasonableness more than anything on Earth, particularly when he notices that, handled by the English, reasonableness has a way of turning out to be to the advantage of England.) This does not happen without some discipline, *i.e.*, some submission of the irrational to the rational. As a reaction, the Englishman is often mad, all the time, or at times, or for a time.

The Russian and the Spaniard also detest objectivity; but when they meet it in the outside world, for, unlike the English, they never experience it inwardly, in themselves. I mean objectivity in action. Hence a contrast between the English on the one hand and the Russian and the Spaniard on the other, at any rate in political and sociological matters; for the Englishman, normally objective, is eminently capable of building up a State, *i.e.*, the system of veins and arteries through which objectivity circulates throughout the body politic; while the Russians and the Spaniards detest the State precisely because of its objectivity. They find it inhuman, cold, odious.

I well remember how some friends of an admirable Spanish novelist, whose books had not yet conquered the public, succeeded in finding for him a nook in the Ministry of Education, where he was paid a modest salary for performing some vague bureaucratic function; and with what moral indignation one of them, referring to his friend's chiefs, cried out to Heaven: "And the blackguards force him actually to come to the office!" A Russian would have been just as indignant.

This illustrates the shade of difference between the English madness and the Russian and Spanish varieties. Normally objective, the Englishman seeks madness as an escape. The Russian or Spanish craziness is more at home and so to speak in its own right, and in both cases as the outcome of a social atmosphere too rarefied for the individual. Here, however, the Russian and the Spaniard, who had travelled together so far, part company. The Russian is no individualist. He is perhaps the least individualistic of all Europeans, as was to be expected of his situation on the border of Asia; for Europe is the individualistic continent and Asia the communal. If, therefore, the Russian finds himself "in resonance" with the ultra-individualist Spaniard it is, however, for a reason quite the opposite from that which makes the Spaniard one of the three crazy Europeans. In the Spaniard, it is the overpowering vigour of the individual pole of his personality; in the Russian, it is that immense plain, that shoreless sea of land too vast to be socially covered even by the strong communal tendency of the Russian.

Their common fascination with madness finds an outlet in their literature. Cervantes is never happier than when he is drawing crazy people—such as his Licenciado Vidriera, who fancied himself made of glass. He delights in that zone betwixt and between craziness and reason where craziness is not yet tragic, and therefore can still be comic. One of his most felicitous moments is when he describes the meeting of Don Quixote, only mad in space, *i.e.*, along his particular and definite North-North-West of chivalry, and Cardenio, only mad in time, as a result of a swallowed-in-fury. Cervantes, however, was himself so sane (though not without his literary King Charles' heads) that he graces with a good-humoured serenity even his maddest scenes; and the same applies to Galdós, a modern Cervantes in more ways than one, also fond of cracked people, yet so lovable and, under the cracks, so sane. To come to the real thing, one has to go to the Spanish painters. El Greco, who painted just like Tintoretto while he was in Italy, went unhinged in Toledo, and there is hardly a Spanish picture of his which can be said to be wholly "normal" or "sane". His tensions are so taut, they seem on the point of cracking. Madness in his art came from the artist himself. In Velázquez, it comes from the subjects which he looks on with his ever luminous and unmoved gaze. In Goya, from both the subjects and the powerful demon in the painter's breast.

These Spanish painters are the true brother-artists of the Russian novelists who have pitilessly explored the abyss of the human soul. Dostoievski, in particular, is both an El Greco and a Goya, for, like El Greco, he shoots up volcanically towards the heights of religious delirium and, like Goya, bursts open the dark recesses of the flesh with his explosive light. There is a poignancy in Dostoievski which is seldom attained by the Spaniards; for the art of the Spaniards stands out on a background of solitude—inward man against outward man (whom he dreams of as the world)—while the art of the Russians is a true torturing and crucifixion of humanity, a stretching of the humanity of a collective-consciousness being drawn and quartered by the four horizons of the endless plain.

Not so with the English, for with them, the background for the crazy individual is a well-defined, medium-sized, well-organized society, with recognized, well-established standards within reach of the odd individual who has just strayed from them and may at any time return to them. Hamlet is the prototype of this kind of English madness. But Shakespeare's world is crowded with them, and it is this social background of the unsocial crazy that makes his abnormal types so fascinating, this weaving of social wisdom into the unsocial raving of his fools and madmen that only an Englishman could conceive and only Shakespeare so perfectly carry out.

So, daring to venture out into the oceans and unlimited plains of the spirit which the intellect is unable to charter, the three mad peoples of Europe, the English, the Russians and the Spaniards, fecundate the three most intelligent and intellectual—the French, the Germans and the Italians. These three latter are the critics, the legislators, the creators and keepers of the rules, the born classics of the European spirit. To them we owe the categories and the forms. Without them, the Russians, the English and the Spaniards would have remained

incapable of moulding their crazy lava into durable shapes.
In their turn, without the Russians, the English and the
Spaniards, the three peoples of the intellect—French,
Germans, Italians—would have remained empty moulds.
To quote de Maistre (in another context) they would
have had nothing but reason. (I am of course exaggerating
both ways, and pushing a *relative* fact to the edge of its
absolute so as to make it stand out more clearly.) Everybody knows the fascination which Spanish subjects exert
on French artists of all kinds, whether writers from
Corneille and even Molière to Montherlant, musicians
from Lalo to Debussy and Ravel, or painters, nearly all
of whom may be said to be sons and grandsons of Goya.
The Germans feed on Shakespeare and on the Russians
since the days of Goethe; Verdi seeks his subjects in
English and Spanish dramatists. Russian authors have
left a deep impress in French literature. Lesser known,
perhaps, is the fact that the liberation of European music
from the strict scholastic canons imposed on it by the
German and Italian masters of the seventeenth and
eighteenth centuries was due, as Manuel de Falla has
shown, to the many years Glinka spent in Spain observing how the Andalusian guitarists, in blissful ignorance
of the masters, had kept alive the tradition of free music.

4

THE SWISS

But what will become of the Swiss? For the Germans, the French and the Italians can import from Russia, from England and from Spain the quota of craziness sane peoples need to carry on in this life. But the Swiss? Blockaded by the intellect, what can the Swiss do—and not merely blockaded but made up of the intellect, made up of German, French and Italian populations. Surely the Swiss must stand in Europe for pure and unpolluted intellect. And, of course, that is what they stand for— which explains that they specialise in the intellectual production *par excellence*—watchmaking.

It is not by mere hazard that watchmaking is a pre-eminent Swiss art. To such an art they were pre-destined, indeed foredoomed, by their geographical situation, in the centre of a ring of intellectual peoples. For the Swiss, by this very fact, are precluded from any velleity to stray from the preordained path of logic. Everything must be with them regulated beforehand, so that one knows what to expect and no surprises allowed. Who knows but that Calvin's success in their land may not be due to some secret resonance between this orderly pre-arrangement of life and the doctrine of predestination. The idea of salvation as the outcome of a life of adventures, sins and repentances, with that dénouement at the end, pending on God knows what unforeseen set of last-minute circumstances, cannot be attractive to the orderly Swiss. Predestination, on the other hand, does suggest a Deity knowing its own mind, really deserving the name of Providence, and keeping a neat file of its creatures in two separate cabinets, presumably with different coloured cards—blue for the elect, red for the damned.

That there is a natural harmony (as Bentham would say) between predestination and watchmaking would appear to be evident. All pre-arranged and no surprises. The spring that is to set in motion the watch-creature or the creature-watch is wound up once for all by the God-watchmaker or watchmaker-God, who, therefore, may be said to have willed beforehand every movement of his creature, since everyone flows from his winding up of the spring. By the way, this simile of the God-watchmaker comes from that great intellect and nothing but intellect, Voltaire, whom a true instinct brought to live at Ferney, as close to Switzerland as a Frenchman can go.

Quant à moi, plus j'y pense et moins je puis songer
Que cette horloge existe et n'ait pas d'horloger.

So he wrote of the world, which he evidently saw as a clock, for he was no Shakespeare, no Dostoievski, and no Cervantes. Still, there is a lot in a watch, in particular two virtues most useful in our modern societies— utility and reliability. Europe trusts the Swiss. They are the keepers of Europe. They keep the European's accounts as they used to watch his house. Swiss are still the Papal Guards, and "Switzers" were the Guards that kept the gates of the Palace of King Claudius; Swiss the troops who fought for whoever would pay them—*pas d'argent, pas de Suisse*, says the French poet—and Swiss are the bankers of half the world; for accountancy, another of the occupations of the pure and undiluted intellect, was, of course, also predestined for the people blockaded by the French, the Germans and the Italians. Nor should we forget the great names Switzerland has given to the highest watchmaking—astronomy—and the highest accountancy—mathematics; for Swiss were the four Bernouillis and the great Euler.

It happens, moreover, that every nation tends to produce as exceptions outstanding anti-types of its own normal type. Thus France, the country of measure, produced that creator of monsters and giants—Rabelais. We must expect to find in Switzerland one or two anti-types to the watch and the clock—rebels to all order but their own. And so we do.

There is, to begin with, Rousseau, the most cracked of Europeans, so cracked indeed that he has left enough nonsense to fertilize at least a couple of centuries of European life, and we all still live, and die, on his diet of sophisms. This Rousseau, with his oriental turban over his progress-ridden head, his illegitimate children shoved into Foundling hospitals and his manuals on education, his anarchistic behaviour and his totalitarian State, his loose morals and his strict morality, his musical talent and his lack of taste, his wandering ways and his persecution mania, his deceitful lies and his shameless confessions, this Rousseau what is he but a watch unscrewed, unwheeled and unspringed, lying in pieces on the table of Voltaire's God-watchmaker for every man to see how poor is the material with which the God-watchmaker can make a watch?

Notice the spring, however. First-class. That spring it was that made of Switzerland through Rousseau the epicentre of all the earthquakes, *i.e.*, of all the jumps in our watches which we have experienced and shall still experience for some time since the first was wound up. And then, there is that other grand crackbrained Swiss—Paracelsus—whose very name is a lunatic asylum let loose: Philippus Aureolus Theophrastus Bombastus von Hohenheim. Who could have thought of that? And in Switzerland, of all places. Now note how evenly has Providence supplied the relief from watchmaking to French-speaking and German-speaking Switzerland, for Philippus Etcetera (not forgetting, though, that Bombastus which is essential) is as Germanic as Rousseau is Gallic, and von Hohenheim is as highfalutin, feudal, arrogant, Teutonic, as Rousseau's "citoyen de Genève" is democratic and republican French.

Both are Swiss enough for all that. Both suffer from that *dromomania* or *Wanderlust* which is less a search for the new than a flight from the old—the old, old self, always the same, always turning round itself like a watch. And yet, as by a kind of compensation, both are bold champions of the sovereignty of the self. Thus Rousseau: "The truly free man wishes only what he can do, and does what he likes." "Expect from me no long moral precepts. I have but one to give you: be a man." And Paracelsus: "Let no one belong to another who can belong to himself." Both incarnate one of the typical European attitudes in their independence of anyone else's opinion, their eagerness to dissent, to find out for themselves, to appeal to nature. That nature, which was for Rousseau the chief mistress and muse, was for Paracelsus the carrier of light. "In the light of nature" is his favourite phrase. And his humanism, deeper in this than Rousseau's, came from the belief that only in man did divine light manifest itself directly.

It may be possible to discern here one of the chief qualities of the Swiss people; a kind of earnestness rooted in a religious spirit. This might well be a gift peculiar in hillmen, for whom the upward rhythm of the high peaks spontaneously orientates the spirit towards Heaven. One must have seen, on the evening of August 1st, the National Day, the groups of Swiss peasants around their homely lights, which like human stars constellate the landscape, consecrating their souls to Heaven, in order to realize the depth and the purity of this singular nation which with so scant material elements and by dint of its unaided spirit has been able to preserve its independence in the midst of this Europe of which it is a faithful cell and image.

5

THE RHINE

FROM Switzerland, centre of Europe, cell of Europe, for, like Europe, she is one and several, the Rhine flows towards the North Sea. The Rhine and the Danube are the two axes of co-ordinates of that figure—Europe. The Rhine divides the Teutonic from the Latin world; the Danube brings Asiatic influences to the very core of Europe and enables European life to flow to the edge of Asia.

The French and the Germans have quarrelled for centuries over the Rhine. *Die Wacht am Rhein* became a sacred anthem for the Teutons, the Gallic reaction to which might well be Alfred de Musset's "*Nous l'avons eu votre Rhin allemand.*" And yet, *pace* Musset, it is doubtful whether "Rhin allemand" is a correct description of one of the two most European of rivers. It is born Swiss, quite Swiss. For many miles from its source it flows in its true rôle, as a frontier, first between Austria and Switzerland, then between Germany and Switzerland, later between Germany and France; and again near the sea, it is Dutch, quite Dutch. Quite German, the Rhine will only consent to be for less than half of its course.

This is what was to be expected of so good a European. As a matter of fact, even in its German section, the Rhine crosses a land rich in European (*i.e.* not *merely* German) traditions, the very heart of Charlemagne's

M

empire; the region of Aix-la-Chapelle and Cologne, Roman cities in German lands, the core of that middle Kingdom which the Partition of Verdun (843) attributed to the elder brother of the three grandchildren of Charlemagne. This territory was neither French like that granted to Charles the Bald, nor German like that Lewis received. It was the centre, the bridge, the truly European heart, which characteristically enough included both Aix-la-Chapelle and Rome.

Now, this is precisely what the Rhine has remained— the spine of Europe, between the Germanic and the Latin worlds; the artery along which live the peoples that refuse to choose between Latin and Teutonic: the Swiss, the Alsatians and Lorrainers, the Luxemburgers, the Belgians and the Dutch (up to a point, though less so, the German Rhinelanders). All these regions, despite the differences of language, history and landscape, evince a number of features in common. The men are particularly tough and stubborn, as was to be expected of "frontier tribes" inured to attacks on both sides; all speak their language—whether German or French— with a peculiar accent of their own; all have left their mark in the chief European pursuits, chiefly in science and in trade. Thus the Rhine-valley turns out to be the home of the most European of peoples: those who, sharing in the gifts of the two great branches of Central and Western Europe, the Germanic and the French, and able therefore to understand both, have proved themselves well endowed in two typically European features —the will and the intellect.

Let whoever doubt it reflect on the intellectual life of such a city as Basle, in which (to quote only from memory) lived and worked Holbein, Erasmus, the

Bernouilli family of mathematicians, Euler, the two Burckhardts (Jacob and Carl), Jaspers, Barth—what city of its size could vie with it in European splendour? And yet, look at the other end, look at the Netherlands, the estuary, so to speak, of that Rhine which cuts Basle in two and which is itself cut in two by Dutch soil—and there again, Erasmus, Rembrandt, Descartes, Spinoza, Huyghens, and, in more recent days, Lorentz.

Nor is this all. For in a way, with but a little imagination, Great Britain may be seen as an Island in the estuary of the great European river, since Britain is also one of those lands which have remained, so to speak, neutral, between the Teutonic and the Latin wings of the European spirit. Even though Great Britain has impressed this axial form of European life with her own particular genius, the "Rhine" remains essentially beyond the North Sea what it has been all along since Basle—a neither-this-nor-that, strong in will and in intellect, keen on realization rather than on argument, ready to compromise, not to submit.

Italy is by no means absent from the Rhine. How could she be? Through imperial Rome, she had been there before any other European nation; and through Christian Rome, she led the conversion of the Rhinelanders to Christianity, which amounts to their conversion to civilization. From that day, the presence of Italy in the Rhine is assured by the Papacy; and the visits of Charlemagne and of Otto I to Italy, in order to be crowned, strengthen the link which later Charles V will confirm. Charles V brings in Spain, or rather makes Spanish influence in the Rhineland official and stately. For the Netherlands, or *Flanders* as the Spaniards said in those days, had developed commercial relations with Spain at an earlier date. The great fairs of Medina del Campo, then the chief business centre of the Peninsula, were held at dates related with those of Antwerp and Bergen-op-Zoom. Flanders bought most of the Spanish wool clip. Wealthy Spaniards slept on sheets of "Olanda", *i.e.*, Dutch linen, and the Flemings were too fond of Spanish wine to let the ships return empty.

So, when Charles, the son of Philip the Handsome of Austria-Burgundy and of Joan of Castille, inherits at seventeen all the thrones of Spain[1] except Portugal, his Flemish friends were elated, for they knew that Spain was wealthy, even before the wealth of the Indies began to pour in, as those among them who had come earlier to Spain in the century with Philip the Handsome knew full well. The King was young and not very intelligent yet, for Charles V developed very slowly; he made every possible mistake; gave all political power to the Fleming Chièvres, the Speakership of the Castillian parliament and the Chancery of Castille to the Fleming Sauvage and, perhaps worst of all, the see of Toledo to Chièvres' nephew, nineteen-year-old de Croy. The Flemish group proceeded to fleece Spain thoroughly and openly, loads and loads of ill-gotten wealth leaving the country for Flanders. The golden "doubloons of two", so known because they were two-faced, were so thoroughly sought by Chièvres that they disappeared from Spain, which gave rise to the taunt:

> God save you, doubloon of two,
> Since Chièvres, so far, has not got you.

The inconsiderate attitude of the young King towards the Cortes ended in a true revolution. What the "Commoners" wanted was freedom, parliamentary

[1] In those days, the word "Spain" included Portugal.

rights, no foreigners in office and no royal bribery of the members of Parliament by offices under the Crown or other worse means. The King appointed the Dutchman Adrian of Utrecht as Regent and left for Germany to be crowned emperor. Though some noblemen sided with the Commoners, one, their first commander, betrayed them to the Emperor. The "Imperials" defeated the Commoners at Villalar (1521). In this civil war, led and instigated by the Flemish advisers of Charles, many cities suffered at the hands of the imperial troops, and in particular, Medina, then a rich financial city, was thoroughly looted and burnt to ashes. The three leaders of the Commoners, Padilla, Bravo and Maldonado, were beheaded. Repression was harsh and even five years after the rebellion had been crushed, Charles V, who had returned with his Flemish cohort and 4,000 German troops, still had a commoner executed.

This crisis determined the history of Spain for many centuries. It saddled Spain with a supremacy of an imperious nobility over the middle class, and delayed by four hundred years the rise of a liberal bourgeoisie which might have seized power already in the sixteenth century. These events, in which the responsibility of the Flemings was so heavy, prepared the terrible fate which the imperial and imperious Spain they had helped to bring about was to visit on them for over a century. Padilla, Bravo and Maldonado explain Egmont, Horn and Montigny. Adrian of Utrecht explains the Duke of Alba. It was by no means a tit for tat; but it certainly was historical Kharma.[1]

---

[1] It should be pointed out that the army of the Duke of Alba was composed as follows: Spaniards: 7,900; Germans: 16,200; Dutchmen and Flemings; 9,600; Walloons: 20,800. The Spanish contingent was 14 per cent.; the "native" over 50 per cent.

Charles, grown so Spanish with the years that he would speak no other language than that Castillian he had learnt last of all, abdicated in 1555-6, leaving Flanders to his son Philip, who succeeded him as King of Spain, and not to his brother Ferdinand, who succeeded him as Emperor of Germany. This decision was disastrous for Spain, for it spelt ruin for her Treasury, enmity with the Northern, Protestant world, and exhaustion in a long war irrelevant to her inherent destinies and interests; for Flanders, it spelt a long-drawn struggle often bloody and destructive—but freedom at the end. The paradox may be put forward that, had Charles V left what then was known as "lower Germany" to the Emperor, it is at least doubtful whether Holland and Belgium would exist to-day.

They do exist, and both with strong links with Spain. History is still often taught in Holland and Belgium with the fierce anti-Spanish bias one might expect in the seventeenth century—with no mention whatever of the Flemish and Dutch domination of Spain during the first years of Charles V's reign. I had the strange experience of informing Dutch university students in 1950 that their countryman Adrian had been not only Regent of Spain but Inquisitor General as well. They had never heard of it. Nor did they know either that Erasmus had lived for years on a pension of 200 ducats paid him by the Archbishop of Toledo, Fonseca. Nor that Erasmus' friend Luis Vives, one of the most enlightened of humanists, expelled from England by Henry VIII for his views on the famous Divorce, had settled in Bruges, at the request of the City, where he had written a kind of Beveridge Report, astonishingly modern in its outlook and conclusions.

But, worse than this ignorance of a number of relevant facts is the wrong perspective that fails to realize that Spain never oppressed the Netherlands. Both Spain and the Netherlands were oppressed by a dynasty which the Flemings and Dutch saw as Spanish and the Spaniards as Flemish. The first day I sat in Geneva as the representative of the Spanish Republic, and when I had just finished a short address during a debate of the European Commission, a red-haired gentleman rose from the bench opposite, walked round the whole room and came to shake my hand most cordially. "I am Colijn"—he said—"the Dutch Prime Minister"; and after a few obliging words on what I had just said, he added: "I had been wanting to meet you to tell you how much I enjoyed your book *Spain;* in particular, all you say on Philip II. It is a subject on which we Dutchmen can still benefit by hearing another point of view." I, then, without the slightest suggestion of humour and with the utmost gravity, replied: "Mr. Prime Minister, we Spaniards are apt to be quite impartial on Philip II, who, for us, was a Dutchman". He reeled, and I thought it Christian to drop a few remarks of bulk without importance, so he could lean on them to restore his balance.

But the fact is that the linen-hair and the water-eye of Philip II could hardly have been less Spanish. When Egmont went to Spain (1565) with reasonable proposals from Margaret of Parma for pacifying the Netherlands, Philip II called a meeting of theologians to advise him on whether he could grant freedom of conscience to his northern subjects. The meeting advised that in view of the state of the Provinces and of the evils which the Universal Church might undergo from a possible rebellion there, the King could grant them freedom of worship without danger for his royal conscience. The King remained adamant.

This King had Lanuza, the Chief Justice of Aragon, arrested on December 19th, 1591, in Zaragoza in exactly the same treacherous way in which he had Egmont and Horn arrested in Brussels on September 9th, 1567, and had him beheaded just as illegally, perhaps even more so. His absolute power in Spain—and, through Spain, in Flanders—came from the defeat of the Spanish Commoners in the previous reign. It was not Spain but Philip II who oppressed the Dutch and the Flemings; and, paradoxical though it may sound, it was Spain's refusal to grant Philip II the funds he needed to wage his Northern wars that, by driving Philip's unpaid troops to mutiny, so terribly increased the sufferings of Flanders.

Flanders had been growing more and more Spanish from the beginning of the century. Waves after waves of expelled Spanish Jews arrived in Antwerp and Rotterdam, and contributed to give to the Netherlands that peculiar Spanish flavour they have not yet lost; and the armies of occupation, not always mutinous, nor destructive, left their mark on the population of the two countries. Indeed, I was witness to a conversation in Geneva, when Dr. Goebbels explained his un-"Aryan" looks by this somewhat unorthodox intervention of the Spanish soldiery in the population of the German *Bezirk* whence he hailed, which, he said, had belonged to Flanders in the past.

Thus did a pure caprice of history bring in Spain at the lower end of the Rhine valley as if to complete its European spirit. There were certain features common to both peoples, the Spanish and the Flemish, which rendered the process more fertile than it would otherwise have been—and in particular, an eye for painting. The Spanish rulers of the two countries were able to choose among their Northern or their Southern subjects some of the greatest names in this art. Rubens, meeting Velázquez in Madrid, studying and copying Titian in and for the Court of Philip IV, turned by Isabel, Ferdinand and Philip of Spain into a Spanish diplomat as well as a Court painter, is a symbol of this connection. Yet another is the close relationship between the Flemish and the Spanish schools of music.

All was not blood, torture and tyranny between Flanders and Spain. When the Spanish guards in the streets of Brussels seized hold of an undesirable passerby, a heretic, a "gueux", or perhaps a thief or a drunk, and took him to the Police jail, they would say to him: "Come along, friend", "Vamos, amigo". The Police Station in Brussels is still named "l'Amigo", and the street in which it is bears still the name "Rue de l'Amigo".

6

THE DANUBE

THE other great European river, born in the high German lands tucked away in an angle of the upper Rhine, flows South East. First German, then Austrian, Czech, Hungarian, Serbian, Roumanian, Bulgarian and Roumanian again, the Danube lends itself obligingly to act as the frontier between several of all these peoples, and, what is more important, as the avenue along which Europe goes towards the East and the East comes towards Europe.

For, essentially, "the East" for Europe is the South East—Asia Minor and behind it, Persia, India and China. Dead East, Europe looks at Russia which is either European itself or Siberian. No real "East". The Danube, a string of South-Eastern capitals—Vienna, Bratislava, Budapest, Belgrade, Bucarest—is the great eastern avenue, and, though in strictly geographical terms its estuary opens out close to Constanza into the Black Sea, historically and spiritually the Danube ends in Constantinople.

After all, the Sultan of Turkey was still the nominal, and in some cases the effective, sovereign of many Balkanic lands in the nineteenth century, and there are still Muslim Europeans in Albania, Yugoslavia and other regions of the Danubian valley. One senses

Constantinople already in Vienna—for instance in the soft expectation of *baksheesh* one meets throughout the day from servants, porters and liftboys who would nowhere else dream of such a thing. In a sense, Vienna and Constantinople were, and probably remain, the two poles of the Danubian region, so that, on the dissolution of the Turkish Empire, some sort of structure with Vienna for its capital was bound to suggest itself. The failure of the House of Habsburg to consolidate such a structure, its tragic incapacity to get rid of the Austro-Hungarian framework, does not alter the fact that Vienna should be the natural capital of the Danubian region.

The dissolution of the Habsburg Empire is often written down to the debit of the first world war; it was in fact one of its causes. The Habsburg Empire fell to pieces mainly for two reasons: the unyielding character of the small clique of Austrian and Hungarian aristocrats who would not share the plums of office with Czechs, Croats, Slovenes and Poles; and the pernicious theory, still abroad, still doing much harm and hatching worse evils, that identifies State, nation and language. Some day Europe may become enlightened enough to realize how inestimable it is for a nation to be composed of peoples speaking different languages. We were not as enlightened as all that in 1918. We thought that it was best for every language to have its own State.

The lower Danube is still in Europe a region of men whose main vigour comes, so to speak, from below the diaphragm. It is the world of strong, nay fierce, virile passions, which seek their outlet in civil and international strife. That protracted Turkish occupation has prevented it from evolving in the same rhythm as the rest of Europe, and, according to national character, has fostered either a fatalistic conformity or the habit of conspiratorial and violent reactions against all rulers. The predominance of the peasantry makes of it one of the most picturesque regions of Europe, and a paradise for the folklorist—a paradise perhaps now lost.

It is characteristic of the spirit of Europe that while the Rhineland looks towards the river estuary and the sea, the Danube-land turns its back towards its estuary and looks towards Vienna. These are not facts that can be proved by statistics, arguments or dates of battles. One has to sense them, and stand or fall by what one senses. Despite the break up of the Austrian Monarchy (and reserving of course what may happen in our future, after a time so pregnant with change) Vienna has remained the centre of the Danubian world very much as Paris that of the rest of Europe. This may well be due to certain features common to both Paris and Vienna. These two cities are essentially feminine in the realm of culture, though Paris, for reasons to be mentioned anon, has often played a masculine part in the realm of politics —the part, one might say, of a masculine-minded woman, such as Catherine of Medici, or Catherine of Russia. Both Vienna and Paris are feminine because both, in the highest degree, possess the gift of form. They differ in that Paris prefers to give form to intellectual, Vienna to emotional, raw materials. Hence Paris brings forth, breeds and matures literature, while Vienna brings forth, breeds and matures music. This, by the way, explains the outbursts of masculine energy in Paris, since she handles ideas, the powerful motive forces of political action.

Vienna, meanwhile, draws to itself the violence, the

virile, pristine, formless force of the Balkan nations, converging on her up the Danube valley, enriched in particular by the strong rhythm of Hungary. Centuries of courtly life have polished the old city. The musical traditions of Germany and of Italy mingle within her boundaries. Can we wonder that Vienna becomes the musical metropolis of Europe? Here, at one time, Haydn, Mozart, Beethoven and Schubert lived within a short distance of each other in both space and time, and a host of minor talents who would have rendered illustrious any other city in the annals of music. To this day, with Bruckner, Mahler and Schönberg, Vienna has maintained her pre-eminence as the capital of European music.

But, indeed, should not Vienna be the capital of Europe in every way if ever Europe came to constitute itself? Search as you may, you will not find another city that may be described as European in the specific sense of that term, meaning of an all-European nature. Paris is French, London is English, Rome is Italian. True, Vienna is Austrian, but this can be disposed of easily. To begin with, it might be more exact to say that Austria is Viennese; because the country is little more than a hinterland for the city, which suffuses it with its spirit. This spirit, by the way, is not German. The language argument breaks down here as in no other case, with, perhaps the single exception of the Americans and the English, so different, despite their (more or less) common language. Someone asked an Austrian after the *Anschluss*: "How are things going?"—"Oh, very well"—answered the Austrian—"with German grace and Austrian efficiency." There, upside down with typical Austrian irony, is the difference in a nutshell. Germans are efficient to the point of being inhuman; Austrians are human, graceful and inefficient. There is also a certain indifference towards results, the next step, the conclusion of it all. That is why no one has ever expressed the spirit of Austria in general and of Vienna in particular better than Schubert. For Schubert is the most graceful and the most inconclusive of musicians. His lovely melodies seem to delight in a kind of wavering, balancing movement, like that of a leaf or a sheet of paper gently held in mid-air by the upward aspiration of his *Sehnsucht*.

This passive, feminine character of the spirit of Vienna seems to predestine her for the part of capital of Europe. For in her all the trends and varieties of the European spirit find a ready welcome. Germanic and Italian, French and Oriental, historically linked with the Rhine estuary and with Spain—for the Court of Vienna spoke Spanish for nearly two centuries—as Jewish as any European capital, Vienna is already a European microcosm. May her freedom be soon restored and with it that of the European Continent whose natural centre she is.

7

THE SCANDINAVIANS AND
THE SWISS

The Scandinavians have remained outside the Roman
Empire for good and all; and outside Christendom for
longer than any other European nation. The two most
powerful influences that go to the shaping of the European spirit have touched them least. When the Swedes
became Christians the Southerners of Europe had
already ten centuries of Christianity behind them, and
the consciousness of belonging to the Roman Empire
had not fully disappeared from their living traditions.
This explains perhaps why the vigour of the Scandinavians has remained unimpaired in its unruly, indeed,
barbarbous turbulence until so late in the evolution
of Europe. Pirates and raiders, they covered and
terrorized with their expeditions regions as far distant
as Ireland, Sicily and Russia. This outward beat of their
energy was by no means always destructive. Normandy
is a Scandinavian creation, and so is England, both
Danish and Norman. The Faroes, Iceland and Greenland
witness to the creative power of their enterprise.
Sicily still remembers them.

The Swedes reached out as far as Ukrainia. Their
ambition was the longest lived and possibly the
most conscious though not the most constructive in

Scandinavia. Thereafter, the wave of Scandinavian expansion receded, and the once vigorous and enterprising peoples settled down to a life of rest. Will gave way to mind, force to reason. All to the good? Well, well.

Sheltered by the sea, with just the waist of the Danish-German frontier between them and continental Europe, the Scandinavians have remained in a kind of marginal position, somewhat aloof from the rest. Their past raids have enriched Europe with the influence of the Norman, Danish and Swedish blood and ways they left behind; but they themselves have remained largely uninfluenced at home. Scandinavia is perhaps the part of Europe in which the dialogue between several European strains has been least active. This has by no means impaired their intellectual strength as such. The Scandinavian contribution to European culture is of the highest order. Linnaeus, Svante Arrhenius, Abel and Niels Bohr in science, Ibsen, Strindberg, Brandes in letters, Swedenborg and Kirkegaard in religious thought, belong to the first rank of European life. What the relative isolationism of the Scandinavians from the European debate may have caused is a certain slowness in the mental rhythm of their average people—as distinct from the outstanding minds; and a kind of distance from, almost an indifference to the struggles of European life which explains the strong attachment to neutrality in most of them.

It is this attachment to neutrality which sets up a resonance between the Scandinavians and the Swiss. As usual, of course, each wears his neutrality with a difference. With the Swiss, neutrality is part of the purely intellectual objectivity of the watch. For the watch scans the hours and the minutes with an equal

impartiality for the saint and for the criminal; and the
Swiss are entitled to argue that in international affairs it is
not easy to tell which is which; to be sure, there are
other factors, and powerful ones, more on the surface
of it.   Switzerland is the source of the Rhine, the
frontier-river between the two chief protagonists of the
wars of the past; made up, moreover, of populations
drawn from both sides jointed with a linchpin borrowed
from Italy; an unstable structure that war might destroy.
All this is true and reasonable.   And yet, all this is only
so because, beneath it all, there lives that detached,
almost mechanical, dispassionate indifference of the
watch to anything but the faithful and ever equal turning
round its own axis.   The stress is on *its own*.

There flows thus from Switzerland a river of neutrality
which, in one way or another and with as many shades as
skies and lands it crosses, covers the whole Rhine valley
and bathes that "island in the estuary of the Rhine"—
Great Britain.   The policy of the balance of power—that
discovery on which British reputation for statesmanship
has rested down the centuries—is little else than Swiss
neutrality adapted from the mountains (where it can be
defensive and passive) to the seas (where it must be
active and, if need be, aggressive).   All this stream of
neutrality coming from Switzerland down the Rhine
valley is poured out into the North Sea, which, with the
Baltic, becomes a lake of neutrality bathing the coasts of
the three Scandinavian nations.

In their neutral ways, each of the three members of
the Scandinavian trinity retains a personality of its own.
For the trinity has to resist powerful gravitational forces
which would tear it asunder were it less solidly cemented
by a common sense of its vital interests.   Sweden has a

N

long tradition of relations with Russia in which she played the conquering, indeed, the aggressive, rôle in the past. Through Finland, usually the victim of both her neighbours in this struggle, Sweden penetrated into Carelia, well inside the present Soviet Union; while Swedish memories are still alive as far as Kiev. Poland was for a time almost a Swedish satellite State. In the political field, therefore, Sweden is closely associated with countries now controlled from Moscow, a fact which is bound to exert a formidable stress on Stockholm. Culturally, Sweden has been for long closely linked with Germany, and in fact, the continental language best known in Sweden for a long time was German.

Denmark has a strong anti-German political tradition. Fallen from her past historical power and enterprise, she has become a small nation, which, between the two world wars, had taken refuge in a thoroughly disarmed neutrality: culturally Denmark sought to balance the influence of her powerful and dreaded neighbour by leaning on France. The two beautiful capitals seem to express the respective leanings of the nations over which they preside; Stockholm, a monumental and noble city, luminous everywhere with the light reflected in the ever present water of its canals and lake, impresses the visitor with a certain Teutonic weight and massive abundance. Copenhagen, on a more feminine key, is neat and elegant as Paris and has about it a distinction of line and a delicacy of colour that no other European city but Paris could match.

Norway, for long reduced to a provincial rank by either Denmark or Sweden, has no city to put beside the two lovely capitals of the North. Oslo was little

more than a big village when it took its Norwegian name
to forget the Danish King who re-founded it as Christiania; and is only now becoming a capital in an architectural sense. But in this old Christiania a literature was
developed sturdy enough to interest the whole Europe.
Culturally the Norwegians leant towards England as
much as the Danes toward France and the Swedes
towards Germany. Politically, they were the safest of
the three until the days of the air-bomber and the para-
chute. Their tradition of neutrality died hard; hours
before the invasion of their territory by Hitler, they
were still growling at the British for some offence to the
sanctity of their territorial waters. Neither they nor the
Danes were to spare themselves the sufferings of war
despite their sacrifices on the altar of neutrality. Only
the Swedes succeeded by a combination of luck and of
painful sacrifices of sovereignty.

Despite their experiences, though, and the profound changes in the actual meaning of neutrality and of
sovereignty brought about by the new international
set-up, the Scandinavians remain at heart neutrals. This
is due to a number of irrational factors, in their turn
determined by their physical separation from the continent and by the fact that they are perhaps the most
advanced of all the Europeans in the process of de-
christianization Europe has been undergoing since the
Reformation. The last to come in, the Scandinavians are
the first to go out. They remain European in that they
remain Socratic—eminently so, among the most enlightened of our European family. But their Christian
faith is dying or dead. They are becoming pagan rational-
ists, leading the rest of Europe towards a life ruled by the
enjoyment of Epicurean pleasures. Their social services

are splendid and their co-operatives magnificent. Life is good and uncomplicated. Love with them has already become sexual pleasure or even less than that—the mere satisfaction of a biological need.

Could it be then that the Rhine was but the hand of a big watch of rationalism turning over the whole North of Europe—Britain and Scandinavia—marking steadily and coldly the advance and progress of Socratic Europe towards its spiritual death? Perhaps. And yet, though those who say that little faith is left in Scandinavia are perhaps right, who in Europe observes more strictly the Christian principle of respect for man? The three Scandinavian crowned republics are models of collective life for all Europe. They confront Europe with this paradox —which the cases of Britain and Holland do but confirm —that the most successful political communities of Europe are all (with the one exception of Switzerland) ruled by kings. This paradox is easily solved.

Politically wise, the Scandinavians and the Swiss, the British and the Dutch, have seldom had occasion to find fault with their public life; therefore, they have not needed a scapegoat. Those that were monarchies have remained as monarchies; Switzerland, which was a republic, has remained a republic. For, in fact, the only peoples that attach any importance to the form of the régime are those who can make a success of neither monarchy nor republic. Politically unhappy because politically unwise, they now throw away the one, now the other, and are never at ease with either.

All this zone of political wisdom in home affairs fits in too well with the European zone of neutrality for any idea of hazard to be a likely explanation. Political efficiency rests on a subtle balance between ethical sensibility and ethical insensibility. Ethics is the soul of politics. Without ethics politics degenerates into boss-rule. The cause of the vigour and of the realism (as opposed to personalism) of this wise, and incidentally neutral, zone is precisely the ethical sensibility of all these nations, their objectivity. And yet, this objectivity implies a certain indifference towards persons. By means of justice, things are purified from any personal element they might contain. What remains is the pure thing, the res-publica. That is why, at bottom and irrespective of their particular "form" of government, these nations are the most republican of Europe, in the real and etymological sense of the word.

This explains also why we owe to the same zone the most genuine republican inspiration in international affairs. In the era of international wars, most of them "personalist" phenomena, this zone gave forth arbitration, so closely allied with Geneva, the Red Cross, also Genevese, the three International Courts of The Hague and the Nobel Prizes of Oslo and Stockholm—a true map of intelligent and creative neutrality.

8

THE GREEKS AND THE TURKS

SINCE we are all agreed that the two roots of the European civilization are the Socratic and the Christian traditions, Greeks and Turks occupy peculiar positions in the European landscape; for the Greeks are the heirs of Socrates and the Turks were never Christian. It is in fact most doubtful whether the Turks could have been considered as European before the revolution brought about by Ataturk. Their claims to belong to Europe have often been disputed on the flimsiest of grounds—that of territory. Europe, it is argued, ends on the western side of the sea of Marmora, and the Straits. That argument would admit as Europeans the Turks this side of the water and leave the rest to Asia. But things are not as simple as all that. Europe cannot be defined on strictly territorial standards. Some of the most European minds that ever lived—St. Augustine, for instance—were born and lived in Northern Africa. The intellectual and religious movements which the imperialism of Alexander determined in Asia Minor and in Africa brought about a close collaboration between Greek and Jewish thought. Philo, another African, a Greek-speaking Jew, who was born and lived in Alexandria, is the predecessor of the Fathers of the Church.[1] Since we have accepted the

[1] Cf. Grousset: *De la Grèce à la Chine.*

Greek and the Christian traditions as typical of Europe, we cannot exclude Alexander from Europe; neither can we exclude the Turks of Asia Minor on territorial grounds.

But the fact is that the Old Turks had excluded themselves from Europe on grounds more solid. One would search in vain in the history of the Turkish Empire for traces of either the Socratic or the Christian spirit. Of course, the Turks could argue back that Europe has a most disreputable history as a Socratic and Christian continent. The Inquisition, the Bastille, the Star Chamber, the brutal sackings and lootings, shootings and beheadings which blot the history of every European nation, remind us that it is best not to throw stones at anybody. But the crimes of the Europeans were committed against a prevailing faith in the principles of Socrates and Christ: they were crimes of inconsistency. For instance, when the Inquisition was, if not at its worst, still harsh enough in Spain, the Spanish Ambassador, Gondomar, by order of King Philip III, informed James I that the King of Spain would not give his daughter to Prince Charles unless the King of England granted freedom of conscience to his subjects! As for Philip II he wrote to his ambassador in London that freedom of worship could not be denied in England to Roman Catholics "since even the Grand Turk allows the Christians who live in his country to serve the Lord each in his own way."

This last example had to be quoted in all fairness to the Grand Turk who, in this episode, turns out to be more Socratic than Queen Elizabeth, at least in the eyes of Philip II, who, as is well known, was an expert in freedom of conscience. It is a fact that, in matters of faith, the Muslims were always freer than the Christians, though both within Islam and within Christendom cruel wars were often fought for matters of dogma. But one wonders whether the Turks were any more Mohammedan than Christian. One does connect Arabs, Persians, Egyptians and even Spaniards with Islamic thought; but not Turks. Their culture seems to have depended on whatever source of light attracted the eyes of their men of letters—now Persia, now France.

Nowadays, since Ataturk forbade them to wear a fez and made the hat compulsory, they seem to be westernized. In this, Ataturk may have fallen a victim to a widespread error: that of thinking that it is the hat that shapes the head and not the head the hat. Turkish ladies have compressed into one generation the long evolution their Western sisters took centuries to accomplish, and from the harem have gone straight into the University, politics and the Bar. In so far as the leading principles and the inspiration for the Turkish revolution came from Paris and London, modern Turks are entitled to describe themselves as Europeans. Time will show how far they have shaken off the subtler chains of Islam.

Islamic chains, and not precisely subtle, were the shackles with which they kept the Greeks enslaved for centuries. Now, these Greeks were the originators of the Socratic tradition, the true founders of Europe. They share this honour with the originators of the Christian tradition, who were Jews. If we consider that perhaps the main share in the creation of Greek culture was taken by the territory in Asia Minor opposite the Island of Chios (the Ionia of the ancients), and that the Christian tradition springs from Palestine, we come to the conclusion that Asia Minor is the true cradle of Europe.

It is generally asserted that the modern Greeks differ considerably from the ancient ones. The news of this fact—if it be a fact—had reached the American Middle West more than twenty years ago, if we are to believe the story told by a Spanish man of letters[1] about what befell a Greek who with him and a score of other European authors and journalists were touring the United States on a good will mission financed, of course, by an American Foundation. Everywhere they went, there was a civic reception; and in one of these, midway between the Alleghanies and the Rockies, the Mayor was shaking hands with the Europeans whom the leader of the group introduced: "Señor Camba, a Spaniard . . . Monsieur Durand, a Frenchman . . . Monsieur Patridis, a Greek . . .—" "Ah!"—broke in the Mayor—"a Greek! A modern Greek or an ancient Greek?"

Now, despite this space-honoured tradition, it is doubtful whether the idea that the modern Greek differs from the ancient has much substance in it, inasmuch as we have but a vague notion about who exactly the ancient Greeks were except that they were a pretty mixed lot, which is exactly what the modern Greeks are. The mere fact that they inhabit the same land, studded with the monuments of antiquity, and that they pursue the same occupations, seafaring, trade, sophistry and politics, would appear to justify the view that the hellenism of the new Greeks does not differ from that of the ancient ones in quality as much as in quantity, the new Greeks being less creative than the old. Perhaps certain strains of the old have weathered the centuries better than others—Ulysses better than Agamemnon, who was a bore anyhow, or Achilles, whose brain does

[1] Julio Camba in one of his books.

o

not seem to have shone as brightly as his helmet. The Greeks use Greece as a base; but they live in the Mediterranean. Their agile minds predestine them for the two commerces, of goods and of ideas. In the catalogue of *obiter dicta* obligingly devoted by Europeans to Europeans, there is a place for an Italian proverb: "When a Greek shakes you by the hand, you must always count your fingers afterwards." This saying, despite its apparent harshness, merely states the disappointment of the less alert businessman at being outwitted in his craft. The Greeks are perhaps over subtle. They owe this quality-defect to an over-dose of that mixing of bloods in which we have seen the cause of the exceptional development of wit and will in the European; in one word, the Greeks are over-developed Europeans. They stand at the origin of European civilization; and they are perhaps also the witnesses of what the coming phase might be in a European civilization that would overreach itself. .

9

THE PORTUGUESE

No adequate view of the Portuguese is possible unless it starts from the fact that they are Spaniards. For saying this, I have been accused of nationalism, imperialism, and all kinds of other crimes. Two points are overlooked: That the Portuguese themselves always thought of themselves as Spaniards until most of them, though, even then, not all, ceased to apply the word to themselves in the late seventeenth century; and that the Spain that would include the Portuguese would not be the Spain that is left when Portugal is amputated. By saying that the Portuguese are Spaniards we mean that they are Spaniards of the Spain that strove to achieve its unity until the reign of Philip II; "strove" *on both sides* certainly at least until Charles V, who married a Portuguese princess, a Spain that included the whole Peninsula. Of course the Portuguese are not Spaniards of the Spain that was left after the separatist war which began in 1640, just when another separatist war was blazing in Catalonia.

The responsibility of the inept Minister of Philip IV, Olivares, was overwhelming in both these wars; but the chief trouble lay in the political incapacity of the three nations that compose Spain—Catalans, Castillians and Portuguese—to build up *a* Spain. It is useless for the Catalans and the Portuguese to blame and curse the third

partner; either the fault is shared equally by the three
(and this is surely the case) or, if the Castillians must be
held solely responsible, a corresponding hegemony
must be granted to them in the Peninsula. Paradoxical
though it may sound, it is a fact that the legend of a
political superiority of the Castillians has been built up
by the endeavours of the Catalans and the Portuguese to
shake off their heavy share in the responsibility of the
three Spanish peoples for their common failure to build
up a first-rate power in the foremost strategic territory
in the world.

The life of Melo symbolizes this Spanish tragedy.
Melo is one of Spain's greatest historians. His *Historia
de los Movimientos, Separacion y Guerra de Cataluña*, is a
classic. It is written in superb Castillian. But Melo was
a Portuguese, who, born under Philip III, while Portugal
was united with the rest of Spain, died after its separation
under Philip IV. He was as prominent in the army as in
politics and letters; and when Catalonia rose in arms
against Olivares, Melo was sent in the royal army in
command of a Portuguese contingent. But when
Portugal also rebelled, Olivares was seized of a panic lest
the Portuguese should betray the King in Catalonia, and
had a number of their leaders arrested and sent to Madrid.
Melo was one of them. Olivares recanted and gave him
an income bigger than that he had in Portugal by way of
compensation. But Melo would not be soothed, and,
espousing the separatist cause, repaired to London, and
later, to Holland, to assist in the war. He served John IV
of Portugal ably and devotedly. But what became of
him? Envious enemies accused him of a murder, and
though he was innocent, he spent years in prison and
exile and lost his estate. A brief spell of undeserved

imprisonment made of this man (who had served Philip IV against the Catalan separatists) a Portuguese separatist. A long spell of undeserved imprisonment could not make of him a separatist again. In his prison in Lisbon, he finished his History of the war of Catalonia.

His life illustrates the root cause of the Spanish tragedy: the admixture of personal motives into public matters. This is an affliction of the three Spanish peoples. But, for a number of reasons, the Easterners and the Westerners have endeavoured to localize the trouble in Castille.

Two circumstances have contributed to this process of isolation and elevation of the Castillians: one is their central situation in the Peninsula, which physically pre-ordained them for the rôle of organizers and centralizers of a rather dispersive territory; and the other, the particular shade of character which marks them out among the other Spaniards for such a rôle. I have else-where explained how the peoples of the Peninsula can be classified into three North-South bands: the Eastern, or Catalans, predominantly plastic; the Central, or Castillian, predominantly dramatic; the Western, or Portuguese, predominantly lyrical. The dramatic Castillian, again, seemed more exposed to the dangers, to the achievements and the failures of political ambition.

The Castillian band comprises Basques, Castillians proper, and Andalusians. Of late, the Basques have con-tracted from the Catalans the separatist measles, which the less wise among them are apt to combine with a racial theory of the State. There are in the nooks and corners of the two Basque countries, the Spanish and the French, earnest folk searching historical, geographic and statistical data to rope in every possible Basque in time and space *ad majorem Euzkadi gloriam.* It is, of course, a most retrograde process. It is not blood but history that makes a nation; and the Basques belong to the history of Spain which owes them so much, or to that of France, in which they have not shone so brightly. Nor should any Spaniard object too uncharitably to a foible which is characteristic of all the peoples of Spain.

So far, only the Portuguese have got away with it. This is due mainly to the fact that the secessionist tendencies of Portugal found easier foreign help than those of Catalonia, which enabled the Duke of Braganza to win his wars. The separation thus achieved was strengthened by the huge colonial empire which Portugal possessed and Catalonia lacked. The lure of this Empire blinded Portugal to her true destinies. It was like a heavy weight pulling her away from that Spain that never was to come to a full existence—a Spain of all the Spaniards. Unable to maintain it by her own means, Portugal inevitably became an instrument in English hands; and it is only fair to record that England has made use of this instrument with the utmost wisdom and moderation. The Portuguese colonies, however, were now and then, when occasion demanded, "offered" by England to Germany or otherwise disposed of. Meanwhile, owing to the disproportion between the metropolitan and colonial populations, the population of Portugal is gradually absorbing more and more Negro blood.

Nor is this all; for the disproportion between that little metropolis and that vast Empire has contributed to create a false view of the Portuguese as a people swollen with pride, *finchados,* as the Castillians say, deliberately using a Portuguese word: while in point of fact, they are

delightfully simple and modest—if partaking of the
general Spanish love of the unexpected, dispropor-
tionate and, in one word, absurd. The Portuguese is
more of a dreamer than his brother Spaniards, with the
exception of the Gallegans, who, after all, are Portuguese
who, by dint of separatism from Portugal, remained
under the Madrid Crown. This dreamy tendency comes
from the Atlantic. It will be found in Brittany, in Ireland
and in the West of Scotland. It is due to the sense of the
immensity that lies beyond Europe, and also to the mists
raised by the Gulf Stream. The dreaminess of Portugal
has also helped to keep her separate from the rest of
Spain. She looks West—to the glorious past.

10

THE JEWS AND THE GYPSIES

THESE two peoples, so different in every other way, stand together in their common function as the weavers of the European loom. By their wanderings all over Europe, they act as a stimulant and an inducement to the wanderings of other, more rooted, Europeans. They differ from the Europeans in that their roots are not in space but in time. Mimetic to a degree, they can take on the ways and appearance of any nation in whose midst they choose to settle; but, beneath their adopted looks and ways, their own inherent identities remain intact. In all this, they may be paired. In every other way, they are miles apart.

Indeed, even in their similarity, they differ considerably. The Jew is a wanderer in the manner of a *pilgrim*, as the very word *Hebrew* suggests in the language. His movement has a powerfully directional element, perceptible both in every Jew and in Jewry as a whole. It is this directional element that finds its symbol in the Promised Land. Every Jew has his "promised land", be it the United States, Israel, or a merely personal objective, not translatable into collective terms. This directional element of the Jewish "movement" is so strong that it has led Berdyaev to credit the Jews with the creation of History; and, indeed, it does seem as if

History were but the polarization into a directed flow
à la juive of all the happenings of human life which had
previously turned up here and there in a spontaneous
incoherence. This was to be expected of a people rooted
in time rather than in space, a circumstance which
makes of the Jews a universal people, indeed, the universal people *par excellence*, since they are the least
subject to localism.

There is, however, a difference between the Jewish
and the Christian sense of History: for the Christian,
History proper starts with Christ. It is the Crucifixion
that gives History a unity and, therefore, a sense; for it is
the Crucifixion that creates mankind as one only
family. For the Jew, History has no beginning in the
past; it has an end in the future. The Messianic urge was
satisfied for the Christian by the coming of Christ; it has
remained open and hungry in the Jew. This longing and
this wistfulness is the prime motive of his untiring,
spiritual energy.

Nothing of this with the Gypsies. They are wanderers,
but, unlike the Jews, aimlessly so. They are true
nomads. They have no purpose but to live. Thus, while
the Jews live in the past and in the future, the Gypsies
live in the present. Their traditions are for them but a
defensive armour to enable them to persist in an environment bound to be alien to them and nearly always
hostile; but these traditions have no other significance.
This explains that while the Jews have an immense importance, the Gypsies matter very little—unless they
happen to be Spanish. Why this exception? It would be
difficult to explain. But the fact is that Spain seems to act
as a stimulant for oriental peoples. Both Arabs and Jews
gave forth in Spain many of their outstanding spirits,

and the Spanish Gypsies are incomparably the best dancers in the world. Possibly, the vigour of a soil that has brought forth a kind of men who spring direct from the source of life, as the Spaniards do, was bound to foster a special vitality in a people like the Gypsies, so wedded with the here and now. The remote origin of the art of the Gypsy is Brahmin. Of this no Spaniard can doubt who has heard a Brahmin singing religious chants. But between that remote background and the final blossoming of this art in Spain there have passed centuries of Spanish life which make all the difference between the Spanish Gypsy and the other Gypsies one is apt to find in every European country.

For, like the Jews, the Gypsies have managed to infiltrate almost everywhere in this Europe which they seem to have adopted as their home. Everywhere, they absorb a modicum of local ways and even of local beliefs, yet remain essential nomads, living on wheels and on horseback, undulating as their women do when walking in their long insinuating, colourful skirts; rebellious to all law, resistant to all assimilation, perennially alien and unsettled, capable, despite their inherent weakness, of living even as adversaries of the environment through the sheer fluidity and liquidity of their behaviour.

The Jews have also penetrated everywhere, or nearly. But, it is a strange though hardly surprising fact that the two nations with which they have been most intimately associated have been those through which they have suffered most. Spain and Germany have, at different times, been a real home for the Jews. Spanish and German have become Jewish languages and remain so to a considerable extent. The reason for this curious fact may well be (if I may quote myself) "a subtle feeling of likeness and unlikeness between Jewry and the two contrasting European types. Like Germany, Jewry moves on; but Germany flows in time, while Jewry moves in space. Like Spain, Jewry is unmovable and deeply rooted; but Spain is rooted in space while Jewry is rooted in time. Jewry thus combines the continuous motion of Germany with the stubborn constancy of Spain; it is ubiquitous but ever the same. In the German language, it found a fit expression for its own mobility; in the Spanish language a fit expression for its own permanency.''

These circumstances explain the division of the Jews of Europe into *Ashkenazi*, or ''Germans'', and *Sephardi*, or ''Spaniards''; the first more Armenoid in physical type, more inclined to orthodoxy, and more popular in their way of life; the second more Semitic in physical type, more inclined to humanistic and philosophical studies and more aristocratic—indeed, so exclusive that, as late as the second half of the eighteenth century, it was customary in the Sephardi communities of the Netherlands to expel a member who married an Ashkenazi.

The Jews have contributed to shaping the History of Europe as much as any foremost European nation. Through their financiers and their physicians, they exerted a powerful influence over European princes. The reaction of the people was at times violent and the Jews were massacred or expelled. Spain, indeed, where they had been treated best of all and where they had become most powerful, was the last to expel them, long after England and France. The activities of the Spanish expelled Jews did much to secure the triumph of Holland and of England over Spain. The intellectual zest of both Sephardis and Ashkenazis has brought untold wealth to European culture. To the names of the Spanish Jews, Maimonides and Ibn Gabirol, and of the French Jew, Solomon ben Isaac, who among many others flourished in the Middle Ages, correspond in our own so many great Jews that a complete enumeration would be tedious. Three, however, must be mentioned; because they stand like the three prophets of a new world— Marx, Freud and Einstein.

These three great Jews have shaken the firmest foundations of our old world: Marx by making ideas *relative* to the production of goods; Freud, by making morality *relative* to bodily states; Einstein, by making time *relative* to the observer. The Europeans found themselves on quicksands everywhere. Some, most of them, have resisted the onslaught and sought to reconquer the solid ground of former convictions; but in the process, the Jewish people have suffered the most abominable of the persecutions they have known in their long and painful history.

Whence this persecution? The answer is clear: from the tension between space and time. Every European national is rooted in his soil; the Jew is rooted in his own memories. This creates a tension between the ways and thoughts of the Jew and those of his environment, different in kind, though not in its effects, from that between any two peoples of Europe. When two European peoples are but neighbours close enough to quarrel, they do so and how cruelly! Think then what is bound to happen when the strange people come to live in the midst of the other: the tension is bound to be much sharper and the sparks ever ready to fly about and to set fire to the house. Which, by the way, is confirmed by the fact that Spain and Germany, the peoples into which Jewry penetrated most intimately, were those that made the Jews suffer most.

This is what lies at the bottom of the Jewish question. While the Jews remain isolated, while there are only a few of them about, no harm is likely to occur; but on the day the number of Jews in any given environment become (or seem to become) numerous enough to give the impression of a "foreign people in our midst", war is not more unlikely than it usually is among any two peoples too close to each other. If the Jewish people have suffered more than the others the reason is that they are the closest neighbours of every other European people. And we know what neighbours are.

Unfortunately for European history, Jews will congregate into towns, thus seeming to be more numerous than they are. This tendency has been described as the natural outcome of the several anti-semitic laws preventing the Jews from settling on the land. Though such a factor may have fostered it, the tendency seems inherent in the specific abilities of the Jew, springing as they do from the deepest feature of his character, his loyalty to time, his shiftiness towards space. The Jew is a mercurial type and his gifts are related to the forms of life that require change. Hence his excellence as an interpreter, in every sense of the word. An admirable linguist, the Jew is also an excellent executant musician, actor, businessman, political negotiator, lawyer, theologian, philosopher. Tehse are not acquired professions due to the legal discrimination that, for long, had closed for him other professions such as agriculture; they are innate vocations due to his peculiar gifts.

All this carries its own conclusion—one which the

rebirth of Israel comes singularly to strengthen. The Jews with strong national and religious convictions possess now a home. Those who remain in foreign lands can either mix and melt into their environment or remain Jewish. If they choose to remain Jewish, *i.e.*, different, Jews should avoid giving the impression of being too numerous on any spot. This in its turn is advisable also from the point of view of the nations in whose midst they settle. Intelligent, vivacious, the Jews quicken the wit and the intellectual life of their environment. They act as a yeast for other peoples. It is perhaps to the scarcity of Jews in Scandinavia (only a few years ago Jews were still forbidden to settle in Norway) that may be due the curious sense of slowness the Scandinavians convey. Yeast, however, must remain but a small percentage of the dough. Such is the ransom of the very wealth of life that is in Jewry. The evil effects of the tension, the massacres and pogroms, the vile ghettoes, the twists and fosterings of unsocial tendencies which persecution caused in the persecuted, the even worse effects their own shameful behaviour caused in the persecutors, may all have contributed to obscure the advantages for all of the tension in itself. Europe owes much to the Jews. They have been everywhere a stimulant to a life of enlightenment and relation; their history, through the Old Testament, has become the adopted past history of Europe itself and has provided untold wealth to European arts and letters; and even passively, as a subject for art, the depth and antiquity of their collective soul has given Europe the masterpieces of Jewish portraiture in which Rembrandt conquers space and time by the sheer power of the spirit.

CONCLUSION

So this is Europe. A country of quality rather than of quantity, rich in shades and in tensions, where men have acquired not only neat individual but neat national outlines, so clearly defined that the intuition can express them in one-word symbols, thus: the Englishman, an island; the Frenchman, a crystal; the Spaniard, a castle; the German, a river; the Italian, a foil. All so concrete that any form of life that falls among them, as a ray of light falling on several crystals, takes on different aspects. A word, a tool for the Englishman, is a blueprint of the object for the Frenchman; a mental projectile for the Spaniard; an encyclopedia of the idea it expresses, for the German; an exquisite morsel to be enjoyed, for the Italian. Love, an indulgence for the Englishman, is a bodily argument for the Frenchman; an intelligent game for the Italian: a fire for the Spaniard; a flood for the German; a mystical perversion for the Russian. Thought, an affectation for the Englishman, is a natural function for the Frenchman; a pleasure for the Italian; a speciality for the German; a vice in the Russian and a torture for the Spaniard.

A country endowed with such wealth of spirit that it seems ever intact and turned forward as if eager to overtake its own destinies. From the vast plain sea of Russia,

a sea without shores, it sets in motion towards the West,
passing through the rapids of Poland, to flow later in the
mighty river of the German soul; from the Black Sea,
another current brings to its core the dark Balkanic
passions, to which Hungary imparts a vigorous rhythm,
and these two currents, meeting in Vienna, endow the
world with the treasures of Mozart, Beethoven and
Schubert. From the Mediterranean, the spirit of Europe
gathers to itself the divine light of Greece and Italy; from
the Baltic and the North Sea, the colder and quieter light
of the North; from Flanders and the Netherlands, the
light of homes and families, shining with human warmth
in dining rooms and kitchens—and so, rich and flavoured
with its many lights of forest and cornfield, vineyard and
pasture, the spirit of Europe ever more and more precise,
reaches the West and branching into its three best
defined peoples—of action, England, of thought,
France, of passion, Spain—flows now earthless and
magnetic, as through three electric points—to quicken
America beyond the seas.